Sue & Lew Cook For You

*A Collection of Recipes
Made at
The Old St. Angela Inn*

ACKNOWLEDGMENTS

This cookbook would not have been possible without the efforts of many different people. We would like to thank our Innkeepers, Andrea, Erica, Honey, Mary, and Ruby. Their help in typing, proofing, and compiling the recipes was a major part of the effort. They also helped in the collection and preparation of new recipes.

Several of our guests contributed recipes, many of them on scraps of paper that have lost the original source, therefore they can not be properly acknowledged. Thanks also to all the guests who gave us their input on "experiments."

We would also like to thank the crew of the Layout Construction Company for coming by after breakfast each day and helping out with the leftovers. Although we were skeptical of their evaluations, they did provide a necessary service.

Sue & Lew Cook For You
By Sue Kuslis and Lewis Shaefer
Copyright © August, 2000 by The Old St. Angela Inn
All rights reserved. No part of this book may be reproduced in any form
or by any means without written permission of the publisher.

Published by:
The Old St. Angela Inn
321 Central Avenue
Pacific Grove, California 93950

Phone: 831-372-3246
Toll Free: 800-748-6306
Fax: 831-372-8560
E-mail: lew@redshift
Web site: www.sueandlewinns.com

Photography: Lew Shaefer
Editing: Annette Zayac
Production: Janet Henke

First Printing: August, 2000

Printed by:
Texas Guides, Inc.
Houston, Texas
800-259-7761

Printed in Houston, Texas, U.S.A.

Step into "Grandma's Attic." The Cape Cod Room is decorated in old-fashioned pink and blue florals. The turn-of-the-century walnut antiques and cast iron stove will conjure fond memories of staying over at Grandma's house.

An ocean view and cozy fireplace complements the muted rose and golds of the Bayview Room. Turn-of-the-century oak antiques, a comfortable sitting area, and a Jacuzzi tub complete your getaway.

A stunning antique, quarter-sawn, oak bedroom set decorated in butter yellow and chambray give the Nantucket room a feeling of being in the French country-side. Curl up with a good book on the loveseat or relax in the Jacuzzi tub.

Bed & Breakfast Inns are synonymous with romance, and romance is alive and well at the Old St. Angela Inn. Roses, truffles, premium wines, champagnes, and etched glasses can add to your memorable stay.

However, the crowning glory is our breakfast. Even the locals know that one of the best breakfasts in the area is served at the Old St. Angela Inn. Served in the redwood and glass solarium overlooking the continually blooming garden, our guests enjoy the taste-tempting treats included within these pages.

Recreate the memories of The Old St. Angela Inn's breakfasts in your own home now...

Step into "Grandma's Attic." The Cape Cod Room is decorated in old-fashioned pink and blue florals. The turn-of-the-century walnut antiques and cast iron stove will conjure fond memories of staying over at Grandma's house.

An ocean view and cozy fireplace complements the muted rose and golds of the Bayview Room. Turn-of-the-century oak antiques, a comfortable sitting area, and a Jacuzzi tub complete your getaway.

A stunning antique, quarter-sawn, oak bedroom set decorated in butter yellow and chambray give the Nantucket room a feeling of being in the French country-side. Curl up with a good book on the loveseat or relax in the Jacuzzi tub.

Bed & Breakfast Inns are synonymous with romance, and romance is alive and well at the Old St. Angela Inn. Roses, truffles, premium wines, champagnes, and etched glasses can add to your memorable stay.

However, the crowning glory is our breakfast. Even the locals know that one of the best breakfasts in the area is served at the Old St. Angela Inn. Served in the redwood and glass solarium overlooking the continually blooming garden, our guests enjoy the taste-tempting treats included within these pages.

Recreate the memories of The Old St. Angela Inn's breakfasts in your own home now...

CONTENTS

The Old St. Angela Inn

Breakfast Breads and Muffins

Strawberry Bread

Makes 2 large loaves or 1 bundt cake

3 cups flour
1 teaspoon baking soda
1 teaspoon salt
1 tablespoon cinnamon
2 cups sugar
4 eggs, beaten
2 cups fresh or frozen (unthawed) strawberries
1 1/2 cups cooking oil
1 1/4 cups chopped pecans

Preheat oven to 325 degrees. Grease two 9 x 5-inch loaf pans or one 10-inch bundt pan and one 6 x 3-inch mini loaf pan.

Sift the dry ingredients together. Combine the eggs, strawberries and oil. Add to the dry ingredients. Add pecans. Bake 1 hour or until toothpick inserted in center comes out clean.

Strawberry Butter

1/2 cup butter, room temperature
2 tablespoons buttermilk powder
1/2 cup confectioners sugar
1/3 cup strawberry jam

Blend together.
Store in refrigerator for up to 2 weeks.
Bring to room temp before serving.

Note: This bread freezes well and is an excellent way to use up ripe strawberries. Also a good tea time treat when made in a bundt pan and topped with cream cheese frosting.

Pocket of Streusel Nut Bread
Yield: 1 (16-slice) loaf

Streusel Filling:
1/2 cup firmly packed brown sugar
1/2 cup chopped walnuts
1 teaspoon cinnamon
1 tablespoon melted butter

Bread:
3/4 cup sugar
1/2 cup butter, softened
1 cup buttermilk
2 eggs
2 cups all-purpose flour
1 cup chopped walnuts
1/2 teaspoon baking powder
1/2 teaspoon baking soda
1/2 teaspoon salt

Preheat oven to 350 degrees. Grease a 9 x 5 or 8 x 4-inch loaf pan.

For streusel filling, in a small bowl, mix together all streusel ingredients and set aside.

In a large bowl, beat sugar and butter together. Add buttermilk and eggs; blend well. In another small bowl, combine flour, nuts, baking powder, baking soda, and salt; mix well. Add to buttermilk mixture; stir just until dry ingredients are moistened.

Spread one half of the batter into greased loaf pan. Spoon filling down center of batter and spread to within 1/2 inch of all sides. Carefully spoon remaining batter over filling, spreading gently to cover.

Bake about 55 minutes or until toothpick inserted in center comes out clean. Cool for 15 minutes in pan before removing.

Note: Bread freezes well. This bread is also good made without the streusel filling. If you prefer a date nut bread, substitute brown sugar for the sugar, decrease the nuts to 1/2 cup and add 1 cup chopped dates and 1 teaspoon grated orange peel after the flour addition.

Zucchini Orange Bread

Yield: 2 (16 slice) loaves

Bread:
4 eggs
1 1/2 cups sugar
3/4 cup oil
2/3 cup orange juice
2 cups shredded unpeeled zucchini
3 1/4 cups all-purpose flour
1 1/2 teaspoons baking powder
1 1/2 teaspoons baking soda
1 teaspoon salt
2 1/2 teaspoons cinnamon
1/2 teaspoon cloves
2 teaspoons grated orange peel
1/2 cup chopped nuts, if desired

Glaze:
1 cup powdered sugar
2-3 teaspoons orange juice

Preheat oven to 350 degrees. Grease and flour bottoms only of two 8 x 4 or two 9 x 5-inch loaf pans.

In a large bowl, beat eggs until thick and lemon colored; gradually beat in sugar. Stir in oil, 2/3 cup orange juice and zucchini. Stir in remaining bread ingredients; mix well. Pour batter into greased and floured pans.

Bake 45-55 minutes or until toothpick inserted in center comes out clean. Cool 10 minutes; remove from pans. Cool slightly.

In a small bowl, blend glaze ingredients, adding enough orange juice for desired spreading consistency. Spread over warm loaves. Cool completely. Wrap tightly and store in refrigerator.

Note: As with most quick breads, this bread stores well in the freezer.

Sweet Cinnamon Quick Bread

Yield: 1 (12-slice) loaf or 3 mini loaves

Bread:
2 cups all-purpose flour
1 cup sugar
4 teaspoons baking powder
1 1/2 teaspoons cinnamon
1/2 teaspoon salt
1 cup buttermilk
1/3 cup oil
2 teaspoons vanilla
2 eggs

Streusel:
2 tablespoons sugar
1 teaspoon cinnamon
2 teaspoons margarine or butter, softened

Preheat oven to 350 degrees. Grease and flour bottom only of 9 x 5 or 8 x 4-inch or 3 mini loaf pans.

In a large bowl, combine all bread ingredients; beat 3 minutes at medium speed. Pour batter into greased and floured pan.

In a small bowl, combine all streusel ingredients until crumbly. Sprinkle over batter; swirl to marble batter and streusel.

Bake 45-55 minutes or until toothpick inserted in center comes out clean. Cool 15 minutes; remove from pan. Cool completely. Wrap tightly and store in refrigerator.

Note: Many recipes call for small amounts of buttermilk, most of which goes to waste before it can be used. We use buttermilk powder, which can be found in the baking products isle at your grocery store. It has a very long shelf life and is easy to use.

Pumpkin Apple Bread
Makes 12 slice loaf

Bread:
1/4 cup vegetable oil
4 tablespoons butter, melted
3/4 cup sugar
1 egg
1 cup canned pumpkin
1 cup finely chopped unpeeled apple
2 cups flour
1 teaspoon baking soda
1/2 teaspoon baking powder
1/4 teaspoon salt
1/2 teaspoon cinnamon

Topping:
2 tablespoons butter
2 tablespoons sugar
6 tablespoons flour
1 teaspoon cinnamon

Preheat oven to 350 degrees. Grease a 1 1/2 quart loaf pan.

Mix together oil, butter, sugar, egg, pumpkin and apple. Combine dry ingredients then add to pumpkin mixture; mix until well moistened. Pour batter into greased pan.

In a small bowl, combine all topping ingredients and mix until it resembles coarse crumbles. Sprinkle over top of the loaf.

Bake 1 hour. Let cool on a wire rack 10-15 minutes before removing from pan.

Note: This is a very moist bread and keeps well for several days when stored in the refrigerator.

Banana Blueberry Mini Loaves
Yield: 3 mini loaves or 1 regular loaf

1 cup sugar
1/2 cup oil
1 cup (2 medium) mashed ripe bananas
1/2 cup plain or vanilla yogurt
1 teaspoon vanilla
2 eggs
2 cups all-purpose flour
1 teaspoon baking soda
1/2 teaspoon salt
1 cup fresh or frozen blueberries

Preheat oven to 350 degrees. Grease and flour bottoms only of three 6 x 3 1/2-inch loaf pans or one 9 x 5-inch loaf pan. In a large bowl, beat together sugar and oil. Add bananas, yogurt, vanilla and eggs; blend well. Add flour, baking soda and salt; stir just until dry ingredients are moistened. Gently stir in blueberries. Pour into pan(s). Bake 40-50 minutes (mini) or 60-70 minutes (regular) or until toothpick inserted in center comes out clean. Cool 5 minutes; remove from pans. Cool completely. Wrap tightly and store in the refrigerator. These loaves freeze well.

Note: Make sure you use only over ripe bananas for full banana flavor.

Chocolate Chip Banana Bread
Makes 16 slice loaf

3/4 cup sugar
1/2 cup margarine or butter, softened
1 cup (2 medium) mashed ripe bananas
1/2 cup dairy sour cream
2 eggs
2 cups flour
1 teaspoon baking soda
1/2 teaspoon salt
3/4 cup miniature chocolate chips
1/2 cup chopped nuts (optional)

Preheat oven to 350 degrees. Grease and flour bottom only of one 9 x 5 or two 8 x 4-inch loaf pans. In a large bowl, combine sugar and margarine; beat until light and fluffy. Add bananas, sour cream and eggs; blend well. Stir in flour, baking soda and salt; blend well. Fold in chocolate chips and nuts. Pour into pan(s). Bake 55-65 minutes or until toothpick inserted in center comes out clean. Cool 15 minutes; remove from pan. Cool completely. Wrap tightly and store in refrigerator.

Note: This bread is best served the next day. Refrigerate overnight or freeze for later use.

Jamaican Banana Bread
16 slices

Bread:
2 tablespoons butter (or margarine), softened
2 tablespoons cream cheese (or 1/3 less fat), softened
1 cup sugar
1 egg
2 cups flour
2 teaspoons baking powder
1/2 teaspoon baking soda
1/3 teaspoon salt
1 cup mashed ripe bananas (about 3 medium sized)
1/2 cup milk (or fat free)
2 tablespoons dark rum or 1/4 teaspoon rum extract
1/2 teaspoon grated lime rind
2 teaspoons lime juice
1 teaspoon vanilla extract
1/4 cup chopped pecans, toasted
1/4 cup flaked coconut

Topping:
1/4 cup packed brown sugar
2 teaspoons butter (or margarine)
2 teaspoons lime juice
2 teaspoons dark rum
   or 1/8 teaspoon rum extract plus 2 teaspoons water
2 tablespoons chopped pecans, toasted
2 tablespoons flaked coconut

Preheat oven to 350 degrees. Coat an 8 x 4-inch loaf pan with cooking spray.

Beat 2 tablespoons butter and cream cheese at medium speed; add 1 cup sugar, beat well. Add egg, beat well. In a small bowl, combine flour, baking powder, baking soda and salt; mix well.

In a second small bowl, combine banana and next five ingredients (through vanilla), mix well. Add flour mixture to sugar mixture alternating with banana mixture, mixing well after each addition. Stir in 1/2 cup pecans and coconut. Pour batter into loaf pan.

Bake approximately 1 hour. Cool in pan 10 minutes before removing to a wire rack.

Topping: Combine brown sugar, 2 teaspoons each butter, lime juice and rum in a small saucepan; bring to a simmer. Remove from heat, stir in pecans and coconut, spoon over cooled loaf.

Note: For a "lighter" version, use ingredients in parenthesis. This banana bread has a real "island" taste and disappears in a flash.

Sour Cream-Raisin Bread

Makes 2 large loaves

Bread:
1 1/2 cups sour cream
1 1/2 teaspoons baking soda
1/2 cup butter, melted
1 cup sugar
2 eggs
1/2 cup raisins
1 3/4 cups flour
2 teaspoons baking powder
2 teaspoons cinnamon
1/2 teaspoon salt

Topping:
1 teaspoon cinnamon
1/4 cup packed brown sugar
1/4 cup chopped walnuts

Preheat oven to 350 degrees. Grease and flour two 9-inch loaf pans.

In a large bowl, stir together sour cream and baking soda. Set aside for 5 minutes. Add melted butter, sugar, eggs and raisins and whisk until blended. Set aside.

In a small bowl, mix flour, baking powder, 2 teaspoons cinnamon and salt. Add to sour cream mixture and stir until just blended. Pour into prepared pan.

Stir together topping ingredients and sprinkle over the batter.

Bake 65-75 minutes until toothpick inserted in center of loaf comes out clean. Cool in pan for 15 minutes then turn out onto wire rack to cool completely.

Note: For a really decadent treat, serve with cinnamon laced whipped cream!

Sue's Almond Poppy Seed Muffins
Makes 1 dozen

Muffins:
1 cup milk
1/3 cup poppy seeds
2 cups flour
1/3 cup sugar
1/2 teaspoon salt
1 tablespoon baking powder
1 egg
1/3 cup butter
2 teaspoons almond extract

Glaze:
1/2 cup powdered sugar
3/4 teaspoon almond extract
2-3 teaspoons water (to desired spreading consistency)
Crumbled sliced almonds

Preheat oven to 350 degrees. Grease 12 muffin cups.

Heat 1 cup of milk in a small saucepan until simmering. Turn off heat and add poppy seeds. Soak poppy seeds for about 10 minutes.

In a large mixing bowl, combine flour, sugar, salt and baking powder; mix well. Add poppy seed mixture, egg, butter and almond extract; stir until just moistened. Fill muffin cups to 3/4 full.

Bake 16-18 minutes or until just set to touch. Cool muffins in pan.

Mix all glaze ingredients together in a small bowl. Brush each muffin with glaze.

Peach Muffins
Makes 12 muffins

1 (16-ounce) can peach halves
1 egg
1/4 cup vegetable oil
1 teaspoon vanilla
1/2 teaspoon orange zest
1/4 teaspoon almond extract
1 cup flour
1 cup rolled oats
3/4 cup packed brown sugar
2 teaspoons baking powder
1 teaspoon cinnamon
1/2 cup raisins

Preheat oven to 350 degrees. Grease 12 muffin cups.

Drain peaches. Chop 2 peach halves and set aside. Pureé remaining peaches in a measuring cup with fork. Combine peach pureé, egg, oil, vanilla, orange zest and almond extract in a small bowl.

In a large bowl, combine flour, oats, sugar, baking powder and cinnamon; mix well. Mix peach pureé mixture into dry ingredients until just moistened. Fold in chopped peaches and raisins.

Spoon batter into prepared muffin cups. Bake 18 minutes or until toothpick inserted in center comes out clean.

Note: These are very moist and freeze well.

"It Doesn't Get Any Better Than This" Corn Muffins
Makes 12 muffins

Muffin:
1 cup cornmeal
1/2 cup flour
1/2 cup whole wheat flour
1 teaspoon baking powder
1 teaspoon baking soda
1/2 teaspoon salt
1/4 teaspoon nutmeg
1 cup plain yogurt or buttermilk
1/4 cup melted butter
3 tablespoons honey
1 egg
1 green onion, chopped
11 ounces whole kernel corn, frozen or canned
1/4 cup diced red and green pepper

Topping:
1 tablespoon flour
1 tablespoon cornmeal
2 teaspoons sugar
4 teaspoons butter

Preheat oven to 350 degrees. Grease 6 "mega" muffin or 12 standard muffin cups.

Combine in a large bowl, 1 cup of cornmeal, flour, whole wheat flour, baking powder, baking soda, salt and nutmeg. In a medium bowl combine yogurt, 1/4 cup butter, honey, egg, onion, corn and peppers. Add to dry ingredients and mix until just combined. Spoon into muffin cups.

In a small bowl, combine all topping ingredients then crumble over muffins.

Bake 18-20 minutes until golden. Cool for 3 minutes and serve warm.

Note: Great served with Mexican quiche! (Page 36)

Applesauce Muffins
Makes 18 muffins

2 1/4 cups flour
2/3 cup sugar
2 1/4 teaspoons baking powder
1 teaspoon salt
3/4 teaspoon baking soda
1/2 teaspoon allspice
1 cup chunky spiced applesauce
1/4 cup golden raisins (optional)
2 eggs
1/3 cup milk
1/3 cup oil
2 tablespoons melted butter
Cinnamon sugar mixture

Preheat oven to 350 degrees. Grease 18 muffin cups.

In a large bowl combine flour, sugar, baking powder, salt, baking soda and allspice. In a second bowl, mix applesauce, raisins, eggs, milk and oil. Add to dry ingredients and mix until just moistened. Fill muffin cups 2/3 full with batter.

Bake 18 minutes or until done. Brush each slightly cooled muffin with melted butter. Sprinkle with cinnamon sugar and serve.

Note: If you have a Trader Joe's near you, their Chunky Apricot Applesauce or Spicy Chunky Apples are great in this recipe.

Lemon Raspberry Streusel Muffins
Yield: 12 muffins

Muffins:
2 cups all-purpose flour
1/2 cup sugar
2 teaspoons baking powder
1/2 teaspoon baking soda
1/2 teaspoon salt
1 (8-ounce) container lemon or raspberry yogurt
1/2 cup oil
1 teaspoon grated lemon peel
2 eggs
1 cup fresh or frozen raspberries (do not thaw)

Topping:
1/3 cup sugar
1/4 cup all-purpose flour
2 tablespoons margarine or butter

Preheat oven to 400 degrees. Grease 12 muffin cups.

In a large bowl, combine 2 cups flour, 1/2 cup sugar, baking powder, baking soda and salt; mix well. In a small bowl, combine yogurt, oil, lemon peel and eggs; mix well. Add to dry ingredients; stir just until dry ingredients are moistened. Gently stir in raspberries. Fill greased muffin cups 3/4 full.

In a small bowl, combine 1/3 cup sugar and 1/4 cup flour. Using pastry blender or fork, cut in margarine until crumbly. Sprinkle over batter.

Bake 18-20 minutes or until light golden brown and toothpick inserted in center comes out clean. Cool 5 minutes; remove from pan. Serve warm.

Maple Oatmeal Muffins
Yield: 12 muffins

1 cup quick-cooking rolled oats
1/2 cup milk
3/4 cup maple syrup
1/4 cup margarine or butter, melted
1 egg
1 cup all purpose flour
2 teaspoons baking powder
1/4 teaspoon cinnamon
1/2 cup chopped walnuts
Cinnamon and sugar

Preheat oven to 400 degrees. Grease bottoms only of 12 muffin cups or line with paper baking cups.

In a large bowl, combine oats and milk; let stand 5 minutes. Add syrup, margarine and egg; blend well. Add flour, baking powder, cinnamon and walnuts; stir just until dry ingredients are moistened. Fill greased muffin cups 2/3 full. Bake 15-20 minutes or until toothpick inserted in center comes out clean. Immediately remove from pan. Brush with melted butter and dust with cinnamon-sugar mixture.

Morning Glory Muffins
Makes 24 (1/3 cup) muffins or 12 muffins and 1 loaf of bread

2 1/2 cups sugar
4 cups flour
4 teaspoons cinnamon
4 teaspoons baking soda
1 teaspoon salt
4 cups shredded carrots
1 cup chopped walnuts
1 cup raisins
1 cup coconut
6 eggs, lightly beaten
1 cup chunky applesauce
1 cup vegetable oil
1 teaspoon vanilla

Preheat oven to 350 degrees. Grease muffin tins and/or 9 x 5-inch loaf pan.

In a large bowl, combine the first 5 dry ingredients, blend well with wire whip. Add carrots, walnuts, raisins, and coconut; mix well. Add remaining ingredients, stir until blended. Spoon into prepared tins and/or pan. Bake muffins about 20 minutes until browned and bread about 1 hour until toothpick comes out clean.

Erica's Caramel Nut Sticky Rolls
Makes 18-24 rolls

Topping:
1/2 cup packed brown sugar
1/2 cup butter, softened
2 tablespoons light corn syrup
1/4 cup chopped walnuts or pecans

Sweet Rolls:
3-3 1/2 cups flour
1/4 cup sugar
1 teaspoon salt
1/2 package active dry yeast
1/2 cup water
1/2 cup milk
1/4 cup butter
1 egg

Filling:
2 tablespoons butter
1/4 cup sugar
1 teaspoon cinnamon

In a large bowl, combine 1 cup flour, sugar, salt and yeast; blend well. In a small saucepan, heat water, milk and 1/4 cup butter until very warm. Add warm liquid and egg to flour mixture. Blend at low speed until moistened; beat 3 minutes at medium speed. By hand, stir in 1 1/2 cups flour until dough pulls away from sides of bowl. On a floured surface, knead in 1/2 -1 cup flour until dough is smooth and elastic, 8-10 minutes. Place dough in greased bowl; cover loosely with a towel, let rise in a warm place until doubled in size 45-60 minutes. Punch dough down several times to remove air bubbles.

Grease a 13 x 9-inch pan. In a small bowl combine brown sugar, 1/2 cup butter and corn syrup; blend well. Spread evenly into greased pan. Sprinkle with nuts.

On a lightly floured surface, roll out dough into an 18 x 12-inch rectangle. Spread with 2 tablespoons butter. In a small bowl, combine sugar and cinnamon. Sprinkle over dough. Starting with the 18-inch side, roll up tightly, press edges to seal. Cut into 18-24 slices; place cut side down in greased pan. Cover; let rise in a warm place until doubled, 35-45 minutes. Bake immediately or place in refrigerator until morning.

Preheat oven to 350 degrees. Bake uncovered, 25-30 minutes. Cool in pan 1 minute; invert onto a wire rack. Serve warm.

Note: This recipe takes time and effort but the results are well worth it! This dough can easily be doubled so you can have twice as many of these sweet treats.

Cherry Scones

Makes 16 scones

3/4 cup dried tart cherries
1 cup boiling water
3 cups all-purpose flour
3 tablespoons sugar
1 tablespoon baking powder
1/2 teaspoon salt
1/2 teaspoon cream of tartar
1/2 cup butter, softened
1 egg, separated
1/2 cup sour cream
3/4 cup half-and-half
1 1/2 teaspoons almond extract
1/4 cup slivered almonds
Additional sugar for topping

Preheat oven to 350 degrees. Soak cherries in boiling water for 10 minutes, drain and set aside.

Combine flour, sugar, baking powder, salt, and cream of tartar in a large bowl. Cut in butter with a pastry knife until mixture resembles coarse crumbs.

Combine egg yolk, sour cream, half-and-half, and almond extract. Add to flour mixture and stir until soft dough forms.

Turn out dough onto a well-floured surface and knead gently 6 to 8 times. Knead cherries into the dough until evenly distributed. Divide dough in half and shape into two balls. Pat each ball into a 6-inch circle. Cut each into 8 wedges with a sharp knife. Place scones onto a lightly greased baking sheet.

Beat egg white until foamy. Brush top of scones with egg white and sprinkle generously with the slivered almonds and sprinkle with sugar. Bake 20-24 minutes or until the top is light golden brown.

Note: Add currants, mini-chocolate chips, apricots, raisins, cranberries or strawberries instead of the cherries. I leave off the sliced almonds when using any of these and just sprinkle with sugar.

These keep well in the freezer for up to three weeks. After shaping and cutting the rounds, wrap in waxed paper and stack two rounds per freezer bag. Thaw as many scones as you need before baking.

Morning Entrees

Huevos Italiano
Serves 8

1 can of whole green chilies
16 small fingers of Jack cheese
3 cups grated Jack cheese
12 eggs
2 cups milk
1/4 cup flour
1 teaspoon baking powder
1 teaspoon salt
1 teaspoon sweet basil
2 teaspoons crumbled rosemary
Warmed marinara sauce

Preheat oven to 350 degrees. Grease an 11 x 9-inch baking dish.

Cut chilies into 16 strips. Wrap chili strips around fingers of cheese. Place chili/ cheese pieces in bottom of baking dish, cover dish with foil and refrigerate. (This portion of the dish can be done the night before to save time in the morning. Also, if you need to grate cheese it should be done the night before to save time.)

In the morning, beat eggs lightly, add milk and flour; mix until all flour is absorbed. Stir in baking powder, spices and salt. Pour mixture over chili wrapped cheese. Cover evenly with grated cheese.

Bake approximately 40 minutes until puffed and golden on the top. Allow it to cool for 10 minutes before cutting into 8 even squares. Some of the puff will go away as the dish cools. Top with a ribbon of the warmed Marinara sauce.

Note: Excellent served with Potatoes O' Brien (page 53) or potato pancakes.

Cups 'O' Gold

Serves 8

Prepare basic recipe for crepes, page 38
12 ounces sage or regular sausage
1 1/2 cups chopped green bell pepper
1 1/2 cups chopped white onion
1/2 cup chopped pimento
12 eggs
1/2 cup milk
2 1/2 teaspoons salt
1 teaspoon garlic powder
1/2 pint sour cream
1/4 cup minced chives
2 drops Tabasco pepper sauce (optional)

Preheat oven to 350 degrees. Grease 16 standard-size muffin cups.

Make 8 crepes, about 5-inch diameter each. Cut each in half, and place one half into each muffin cup. Ruffle edges.

Prepare sausage mix: Mash sausage into bits. Combine sausage with bell pepper, onion and pimento in skillet and cook over medium heat until sausage turns lightly browned. If a more highly seasoned effect is desired, add two drops Tabasco pepper sauce blended in with the sausage mix.

Prepare egg mix: Lightly beat eggs with milk, salt and garlic powder until blended.

Assemble: Place about 1-2 tablespoons of the sausage mixture into the crepe cups. Place 4-5 tablespoons of egg mixture over the sausage.

Bake 25 minutes. Let sit for 5 minutes. Remove from muffin tin. Top cups with sour cream and chives. Recommend two egg cups per person. Garnish plate with parsley or watercress.

Note: Serve with Green Chili Hash Browns (page 53) for a very colorful and impressive looking plate. This recipe has Ashley's paw print approval.

Pesto Eggs with Leeks and Asparagus
Serves 6

Creamy pesto sauce:
1 cup dry white wine
3 tablespoons white vinegar
2 tablespoons minced shallots
1 1/2 cups heavy cream
1/4 cup fresh herb pesto or bottled basil pesto

Eggs:
4 tablespoons butter
3/4 teaspoon minced garlic
1/4 cup washed chopped leeks (white part only)
6 eggs
2 tablespoons half-and-half
4 tablespoons herb pesto
1/2 teaspoon pepper
16 blanched asparagus tips
3 tablespoons part skim milk Ricotta cheese
2 teaspoons chopped fresh basil
6 slices Italian or French bread or English muffins, lightly toasted

Preheat oven to 350 degrees.

Sauce: In a two-quart saucepan, reduce the white wine, vinegar and shallots to 2 tablespoons of liquid. Remove shallots with a slotted spoon. Add cream and reduce again by one third; stir in pesto and keep warm.

Eggs: Melt butter in medium skillet. Add garlic and leeks. Sauté over medium heat until tender, 1 to 2 minutes. Remove from heat and set aside. Whisk together eggs, half-and-half, pepper and pesto. Melt remaining 2 tablespoon butter in skillet. Pour in egg mixture and cook over medium heat until just beginning to set. Add leeks, asparagus and scrambled egg mixture. Fold in ricotta cheese and remove from heat.

Place the lightly toasted bread slices on a baking sheet; top each with equal amount of egg mixture. Heat in oven for 5 minutes and serve topped with creamy pesto sauce.

Note: Sauce can be made 24 hours ahead up to the point of adding pesto. Reheat before stirring in pesto. To make pesto, place 1 cup fresh basil, 1 tablespoon coarse salt, 1 clove garlic and 2 tablespoons of pine nuts into a food processor and mix until a paste forms. Add 2 tablespoons of grated Parmesan cheese and blend until mixed. With the processor running, add 6 tablespoons of olive oil in a steady stream. Refrigerate or freeze any unused pesto right away.

Baked Eggs and Bacon in Lacy Potato Nests
Serves 6

8-ounce baking potato, peeled
1 tablespoon olive oil
1 tablespoon melted butter
2 teaspoons dried rosemary
1/2 teaspoon paprika
Ground pepper to taste
6 slices cooked bacon
6 eggs
1 1/2 teaspoons basil
1 1/2 teaspoons parsley

Preheat oven to 350 degrees. Line 6 large muffin cups with parchment or tin foil. Brush with oil and butter combination.

Coarsely grate potato into a colander. Rinse well with cold water. Drain and gently squeeze out moisture. Transfer potato to mixing bowl and add olive oil, rosemary, paprika and pepper, stir well. Divide among muffin cups. Using back of spoon, gently press mixture into bottom and halfway up sides of cups. Bake 30 minutes until golden.

Remove nests from oven and sprinkle with 1/2 slice of crumbled bacon. Break one egg in each nest and sprinkle with rest of bacon slice.

Return to oven and bake 15-18 minutes until yolk is set. Carefully remove nests by lifting up on edges of foil or parchment; peel off any foil if needed. Sprinkle with basil and parsley. Serve warm.

Note: Nests can be made the night before. Reheat for 10 minutes to crisp before adding bacon and egg.

Cheese Blintz
Serves 6 (2 crepes each)

Crepes:
1 1/2 cups milk
1 cup flour
2 eggs
1 tablespoon cooking oil
1/4 teaspoon salt

Filling:
1 beaten egg
1 (8-ounce) package cream cheese, softened
1 cup dry cottage cheese
1 teaspoon vanilla

For crepes, combine milk, flour, eggs, oil and salt in a mixing bowl. Beat until well blended. Heat a 6-inch skillet or crepe pan. Remove from heat. Spoon in 2 tablespoons batter. Return to heat, brown one side only. Invert pan over paper towels; remove crepe. Repeat with the remaining batter to make 12 crepes, greasing skillet occasionally.

To make the filling, beat together the egg, cheeses, and vanilla. Spoon 1 rounded tablespoon in the center of unbrowned side of each crepe. Fold crepes with all four sides under to form a small pocket. Place crepes in a 12 x 7 1/2 x 2-inch baking dish with the folded side down. Cover and bake in a 350-degree oven for 20 minutes.

Pineapple-Strawberry Sauce:
1/4 cup sugar
2 tablespoons cornstarch
15 1/4 ounces canned pineapple chunks
2/3 cup orange juice
1 basket (1 1/2 cups) fresh strawberries, sliced

In a medium saucepan, combine 1/4 cup sugar and 2 tablespoons cornstarch. Drain the liquid from one 15-ounce can pineapple chunks into pan, set pineapple chunks aside. Add 2/3 cup orange juice to pan and stir to combine. Simmer over low heat until thick and bubbly, stirring occasionally. When thickened, turn off heat until ready to serve. (Makes 3 cups of sauce.)

Slice one basket of strawberries into thickened sauce. Add reserved pineapple chunks. Gently reheat just before serving.

Place two blintzes on each plate, top with Pineapple-Strawberry Sauce and garnish plate with a sliced, fanned strawberry.

Egg Custard Casserole
Serves 8

1/4 cup butter or margarine
14 eggs
1/2 cup milk
1 teaspoon salt
1/2 teaspoon white pepper
1/2 teaspoon dill weed
1 cup fresh, canned or imitation frozen crab meat
3 ounces cream cheese, cut into small cubes
Paprika

Place butter into a 9-inch glass pie plate and melt in microwave; spread butter to coat bottom of plate.

Beat eggs, milk, salt, pepper and dill weed. Pour mixture into pie plate. Stir in crab meat and cheese cubes. Bake immediately, or cover with plastic wrap or aluminum foil and refrigerate overnight for up to 24 hours.

To bake, preheat oven to 350 degrees. Sprinkle casserole with paprika. Bake uncovered 40-45 minutes or until center is set. This will puff as it bakes but settles down as it cools.

Note: Imitation crab meat is best. Cubed ham or Canadian bacon can be substituted for crab meat with delicious results.

Death by Cheese
Serves 16

12 eggs
1 cup flour
2 teaspoons baking powder
1/4 teaspoon salt
2 cups milk
16 ounces cottage cheese
8 ounces cream cheese, cut into cubes
2 pounds Jack cheese, cut into cubes
4 tablespoons butter (optional)

Preheat oven to 350 degrees. Grease two 11 x 7-inch pans.

Beat eggs in a large bowl. Add flour, baking powder, salt and milk. Be sure all flour is absorbed. Beat in cottage cheese (it will still be in small curds). Stir in cubed cheeses. Make sure cream cheese cubes do not stick together. Pour into pans. Dot with butter. Bake 50-60 minutes, until puffed and golden on top. Cool 10-15 minutes before cutting.

Note: To save time, cut the cream cheese and Jack cheese into cubes, wrap tightly and refrigerate the night before they are needed.

Artichoke Frittata
Serves 8

9 ounces frozen or canned artichoke hearts (not marinated)
1 small onion, coarsely chopped
1 tablespoon olive oil
1 tablespoon butter
1/2 teaspoon dried oregano
1 clove garlic, minced
3/4 cup grated Parmesan cheese
6 eggs
1/2 cup milk
1/4 teaspoon salt
1/4 teaspoon pepper
1/8 teaspoon nutmeg
1 cup grated Monterey Jack cheese

Preheat oven to 350 degrees. Grease a 1 1/2 quart baking dish.

Sauté artichoke hearts, onion, garlic and oregano in olive oil and butter until onion is just soft. Sprinkle 1/4 cup freshly shredded Parmesan cheese over bottom and sides of baking dish. Spoon artichoke mixture over bottom of dish.

Beat together eggs, milk, salt, pepper, and nutmeg. Stir in Monterey Jack cheese and 1/4 cup of Parmesan cheese. Pour over artichoke mixture.

Bake 30 minutes. Sprinkle with remaining Parmesan cheese. Bake 5-10 minutes more, until golden brown. Cool 5 minutes before cutting into 8 equal squares.

Note: Monterey County is the "Artichoke Capital" of the World. The majority of the nation's artichokes are grown in the fertile fields surrounding the Monterey Peninsula.

Individual Spinach Frittatas
Serves 8

2 (10-ounce) packages frozen chopped spinach, thawed , squeezed dry
1 1/2 cups Ricotta cheese
1 1/2 cups grated Parmesan cheese
2 cups chopped mushrooms
1/4 cup chopped onion
1 teaspoon salt
1/2 teaspoon pepper
1 teaspoon oregano
8 eggs

Preheat oven to 350 degrees.

Coat 8 (8-ounce) ramekins with vegetable cooking spray.

Beat eggs in a medium bowl. Add remaining ingredients and combine. Divide mixture equally among ramekins. Place ramekins in roasting pan and fill pan 1/2 way with boiling water. Place roasting pan in oven. Bake 25 minutes until firm, but moist. Unmold frittatas on plate. Serve warm.

Note: We serve this with a potato side dish. Be sure to squeeze the spinach dry or frittatas will be watery when unmolded onto plates. This recipe doubles and halves very nicely.

Winter Quiche with Leeks and Brie
Serves 8

Puff pastry sheet, thawed 30 minutes
2 tablespoons olive oil
2 cups thinly sliced leeks, white and light green parts only
1 small clove garlic, minced
1/4 teaspoon each of dried thyme and sage (use more if fresh)
12 eggs
1/2 cup half-and-half
1/2 cup brie, cut into chunks
Salt and pepper to taste

Preheat oven to 450 degrees. Place pastry in a 9-inch pie plate, trim to fit. Bake 5-10 minutes until crust browns slightly. Remove from oven, decrease oven to 350 degrees.

While crust is baking, rinse leeks well. Shake and dry. Sauté with garlic and olive oil over medium heat until tender, 8 minutes. Remove from heat. In a small bowl, mix eggs, milk and herbs, season with salt and pepper. Into partially cooked crust, spread sautéed leeks and garlic. Sprinkle with chunks of brie. Pour egg mixture over top. Bake at 350 degrees for 25 minutes until quiche is set and top is slightly brown. Cool before serving.

Note: This has a very delicate taste and is a great way to use small pieces of leftover brie.

Vegetable Quiche
Serves 8

1 sheet puff pastry
1 potato, diced
1 small head of broccoli, diced
1 quarter head of cauliflower, diced
2 carrots, diced
1 small onion diced
2 tablespoons vegetable oil
1 teaspoon salt
1/2 teaspoon pepper
1 1/2 teaspoons garlic powder
1 1/2 cups grated Cheddar cheese
8 eggs
1 cup milk

Preheat oven to 350 degrees. Press defrosted puff pastry in a 9-inch greased quiche pan.

Sauté potatoes, broccoli, cauliflower, carrots and onions in vegetable oil over medium heat. Cook until vegetables are tender. Sprinkle 1/2 cup Cheddar cheese on the puff pastry, add the vegetables and cover with the remaining cheese. Set aside.

In a large bowl, beat the eggs and milk. Add salt, pepper and garlic. Pour over vegetable-cheese mixture. Bake 40-45 minutes.

Note: This quiche is so versatile! Any variety of vegetables can be used, dependent upon what you have on hand. Try using mushrooms, red potatoes, zucchini (squeezed dry), tomato slices or asparagus tips.

Mexican Quiche
Serves 8

8 eggs
1/4 cup flour
1 teaspoon baking soda
1 teaspoon salt
1/2 cup half-and-half
4-6 ounces mild green chilies, diced
2 cups cottage cheese
2 cups grated sharp Cheddar cheese

Preheat oven to 400 degrees. Generously grease a quiche pan or 9-inch pie plate with Pam or butter.

Beat together eggs, flour, baking soda, salt, and half-and-half. Add chilies, cottage cheese, and Cheddar cheese. Pour mixture into quiche pan and bake 45 minutes to 1 hour, until firm in center. Serve with black bean or tomato salsa.

Note: Serve with "It Doesn't Get Any Better Than This" Corn Muffins.

Tomato and Zucchini Quiche
Serves 8

1/4 cup Parmesan cheese, grated
4 ounces Gruyere or Swiss cheese, grated
1 small zucchini, grated and squeezed dry
2 tomatoes, sliced
6 large eggs
1 cup heavy cream
1/2 teaspoon salt
1/8 teaspoon nutmeg
1/8 teaspoon black pepper
1 9-inch pie shell or 1 sheet puff pastry

Preheat oven to 350 degrees. Press puff pastry into a greased 9-inch glass pie plate.

Distribute cheese evenly on bottom of unbaked pie shell. Top with zucchini.

Whisk together cream, eggs, nutmeg, salt and pepper. Pour into pie shell. Place tomato slices decoratively on top. Bake 50-55 minutes or until set. Let stand 5 minutes before serving.

Note: This is an excellent way to use fresh summer produce.

Guiltless Strata
Serves 10

1 teaspoon vegetable oil
1 pound or 3 medium red potatoes, thinly sliced
12 eggs (or 5 eggs and 7 egg whites)
1/3 cup flour
1 teaspoon baking powder
1/2 teaspoon salt
1/2 teaspoon black pepper
1 (16-ounce) container low fat cottage cheese (or non-fat)
1/2 cup Parmesan cheese, grated
1 1/4 cups sharp cheddar cheese, shredded (or reduced fat)
1 1/2 cups diced ham
1/2 cup chopped green onion
1/2 cup chopped red bell pepper

Preheat oven to 350 degrees.

Coat a large nonstick skillet with cooking spray, add oil and heat to a medium heat. Add potatoes and sauté until brown and tender, about 14 minutes. Let cool slightly.

Whisk eggs together in a large bowl. Add flour, baking powder, salt and pepper, beat until well mixed. Add remaining ingredients and combine well.

Spray a 13 x 9-inch pan with cooking spray. Layer sautéed potatoes in the bottom of the pan. Pour egg mixture over potatoes. Bake on a rack that is placed in the top third of the oven at 350 degrees, 40-45 minutes, or until golden on top and set in the center. Serve immediately.

Note: A strata is a layered dish. For a different version, see Egg Strata on page 39. If you choose the guiltless route (ingredients in parenthesis), no one will ever guess that this strata is much lower in fat than the regular version.

Carnivore Crepes
Serves 8

Crepes:
4 large eggs
1 teaspoon salt
1 tablespoon vegetable oil
2 2/3 cups milk
2 cups plus 4 tablespoons flour

Mix together eggs, salt, oil, and milk. Whisk in flour until absorbed. Let mixture rest for at least 10 minutes. Generously coat crepe pan with Pam. Pour batter into shallow pie plate. Heat crepe pan to just sizzling. Dip domed side of crepe pan into batter, return to heat. Cook about 30 seconds, flip crepe and cook about 15 seconds more.

Filling:
12 ounces sage sausage
1/4 cup chopped onion
8 large mushrooms, sliced
1/4 teaspoon ground thyme
1/4 teaspoon garlic powder
1/2 cup shredded sharp Cheddar cheese
1 (3-ounce) package cream cheese, cut into small chunks
16 crepes
1/2 cup sour cream

In heavy skillet, sauté sausage, mushrooms, onion, thyme and garlic, stirring to crumble meat. Remove from heat, add small chunks of cream cheese and grated Cheddar cheese.

Fill each crepe with 2 tablespoons of sausage mixture. Roll up and place seam down in two 13 x 8 x 2-inch pans, lightly coated with cooking spray. Cover with foil and bake at 350 degrees for 15 minutes until warmed. Top each crepe with a small dollop of sour cream. Serve 2 crepes per person.

Note: Serve with Green Chili Hash Browns. Crepes can be made ahead of time and kept in the refrigerator in an airtight bag for use with other recipes. The entire filled crepe can also be made the night before. Reheat about 20 minutes in the morning.

Festival Pancakes
Make 10 pancakes

1 cup flour
1/2 teaspoon baking soda
1 teaspoon baking powder
1/2 teaspoon salt
1/2 teaspoon cinnamon
2 eggs
1 cup buttermilk (powdered buttermilk works fine)
2 tablespoons butter, melted
1 tablespoon sugar (optional)
1 large apple, shredded
1/4 cup raisins
1/4 cup chopped walnuts

Combine first 9 ingredients. Whisk until smooth. Add apple. Add raisins and walnuts or use as garnish. Spoon 1/4 cup portions onto a hot grease griddle. Cook until golden on both sides. Serve with powdered sugar and garnish. Syrups may also be served.

Note: The apple provides natural sugar and makes these pancakes very light.

Egg Strata
Serves 8

Sourdough French bread, sliced
Sliced Cheddar cheese (enough to cover 11 x 7-inch baking dish)
Sliced Swiss or Monterey Jack cheese (to cover 11 x 7-inch
*   baking dish)*
8 slices Canadian bacon, cubed
12 eggs
Dash of thyme
Dash of cayenne
1/3 cup half-and-half
1 teaspoon garlic powder
1/2 teaspoon black pepper
Worcestershire sauce (a couple of dashes)

Spray an 11 x 7-inch baking dish with Pam. Arrange French bread to cover bottom of dish. Cover with Swiss cheese. Layer with Canadian bacon. Top with cheddar cheese. In a bowl, combine remaining ingredients; beat until smooth. Pour into baking dish. Egg batter should just cover layers, it will expand while cooking. Cover with plastic wrap. Refrigerate overnight. In the morning, preheat oven to 350 degrees. Uncover and bake 40-45 minutes until browned and bubbly.

Note: Vegetarian version; 1/2 package frozen spinach, thawed and squeezed dry, sautéed with 1 1/2 cups sliced mushrooms in 2 tablespoons butter. Use in place of bacon.

Belgian Waffles with Brandied Peaches and Blueberry Syrup

Serves 6

Blueberry Syrup:
2 cups blueberries
1/2 cup sugar
1/2 cup water
1 slice lemon
1/2 cup light corn syrup

Waffles:
2 cups sifted flour
4 teaspoons baking powder
1 teaspoon salt
2 cups milk
4 eggs, separated
1 cup butter, melted, cooled to room temperature
1 cup pecans, finely chopped

Peaches:
2 cups peeled and sliced peaches
1 tablespoon lemon juice
1/2 cup sugar
2 tablespoons butter
1/4 cup brandy
Powdered sugar for garnish

Syrup: Simmer blueberries, sugar, water and lemon together until they form a syrup, about 10 minutes. Stir in corn syrup, simmer for 3 minutes. Keep warm.

Peaches: In a medium bowl, toss peaches and lemon juice together to prevent browning. Stir in sugar, set aside. Melt 2 tablespoons butter in a large sauté pan. Sauté peaches over medium heat 1 minute. Stir in brandy, ignite or cook on low heat 3-5 minutes. Remove from heat.

Waffles: Preheat Belgian waffle iron. Sift together flour, baking powder and salt. Combine milk and egg yolks. Beat egg whites until they form stiff peaks. Add the milk-egg mixture to the dry ingredients. Stir in butter. Fold in egg whites. Stir in chopped pecans. Pour batter into waffle iron, bake according to manufacturer's directions. Make 6 waffles. Keep waffles warm on baking racks in a low oven.

Assembly: Sprinkle individual plates with powdered sugar. Place waffles on plates. Spoon some peaches into the centers and serve with blueberry syrup.

Note: The blueberry syrup can be made ahead and kept refrigerated. Reheat before serving.

Oh, Those French and Their Toast!

Apple Upside-Down French Toast
8 servings

1/2 cup butter or margarine
1 1/4 cups packed brown sugar
1 tablespoon water
2 large Granny Smith apples, peeled, cored and sliced
1 loaf French or Italian Bread, cut into 1-inch thick slices
6 eggs, beaten
1 1/2 cups milk
1 tablespoon vanilla

Melt butter in medium saucepan. Stir in brown sugar and water. Cook, stirring constantly, until thickened. Pour into a well-greased 13 x 9-inch baking dish. Line rows of apple slices on top of the sugar mixture.

Cut bread into 1-inch thick slices. Place slices on top of apples, filling in gaps with smaller pieces of bread.

Mix eggs, milk, and vanilla. Pour over bread making sure to coat all bread. Cover pan with plastic wrap and refrigerate overnight.

In the morning, preheat oven to 350 degrees. Uncover French toast. Bake 40 minutes. Remove pan from oven, place a baking sheet over the baking dish and invert carefully. Wait 3 minutes and lift off the baking dish. Cut into 8 squares.

Note: Peaches are also delicious in this French Toast. Reserve the liquid from a 29-ounce can to make Peach Syrup. To make Peach Syrup, add enough orange juice to peach juice to make two cups. Mix in 3 tablespoons of cornstarch and 1 teaspoon of lemon extract. Stir over low heat until thickened.

French Toast with Caramelized Pecans and Blueberry Sauce
Serves 8

Sourdough bread sliced into 1" thick slices
10 eggs
1 1/2 cups of milk
1/2 teaspoon nutmeg
1 tablespoon vanilla
1 cup packed brown sugar
Powdered sugar for garnish

Topping:
1 teaspoon butter
1/4 teaspoon salt
1 cup pecans
1/2 stick butter
1/4 cup packed brown sugar

Blueberry Sauce:
1/2 cup maple syrup
1 cup blueberries
1 tablespoon lemon juice

Grease an 11 x 7-inch baking dish with cooking spray. Place a single layer of sliced bread in baking dish.

In a large bowl, mix the eggs, milk, nutmeg, vanilla, and brown sugar. Pour over the bread. Cover and refrigerate overnight.

In the morning preheat oven to 350 degrees.

Toast the pecans on a baking sheet about 10 minutes. In a sauté pan on low heat, toss toasted pecans with 1 teaspoon butter and 1/4 teaspoon salt. Top refrigerated bread with toasted pecan mixture.

In sauté pan, melt 1/2 stick of butter with 1/4 cup brown sugar. Drizzle over the French toast. Bake 40 minutes.

Blueberry sauce: Place maple syrup and blueberries into a saucepan. Heat on low until the blueberries burst. Add lemon juice just before you are ready to serve.

To serve, sprinkle French toast with powdered sugar and top with blueberry sauce.

Orange Croissant French Toast
Serves 6

4 *eggs*
5 *ounces evaporated milk*
1/3 cup orange juice
1 tablespoon sugar
6 croissants, split in half

In a small bowl, combine eggs, evaporated milk, orange juice and sugar. Dip each croissant half into egg mixture, coating thoroughly. Place slices in a single layer on a foil-lined baking sheet.

To bake, place baking sheet in a 450 degree oven for 6 minutes or until light browned. Turn and bake an additional 6 minutes.

OR

On a heated and greased griddle, cook croissants 4 minutes per side until golden brown.

Serve with Honey Orange Syrup.

Honey Orange Syrup:
(Makes 1 1/2 cups)
2 tablespoons water
3/4 cup packed brown sugar
1/2 cup orange juice
1/2 cup butter
2 tablespoons maple syrup
4 tablespoons grated orange peel
1/2 cup honey

In a small saucepan, boil water, sugar and orange juice. Add butter, maple syrup and orange peel. Add honey; blend well. Serve warm.

Note: The French toast freezes very nicely. Place in freezer bags and seal tightly. Thaw before cooking. The syrup will keep for up to one month in a covered container stored in the refrigerator.

Raspberry-Almond Croissant French Toast
Serves 6

6 croissants

Stuffing:
1/2 cup mascarpone
1 cup ricotta cheese
1/4 cup almond paste
2 cups raspberry preserves

Egg Batter:
6 eggs
1/2 cup heavy cream
1 teaspoon almond extract
1/4 cup sliced almonds
2 tablespoons corn oil
2 tablespoons butter

Topping:
1/4 cup mascarpone
2 tablespoons amaretto
1/4 cup fresh raspberries

Preheat oven to 350 degrees.

With an electric mixer, blend together mascarpone and ricotta. Split each croissant. Spread each with 1/6 of almond paste, raspberry preserves and cheese mixture.

Whisk together eggs, cream and almond extract. Dip croissants in egg mixture. Dip each croissant into sliced almonds.

Over medium heat, melt together butter and corn oil in large skillet. Sauté croissants until lightly browned, about 4 minutes. Turn and brown the other side. Place croissants in oven for about 5 minutes to heat through.

Whisk together mascarpone and amaretto. Serve French toast with dollop of mascarpone/amaretto mixture and fresh raspberries.

French Toast Sundae
Makes 6 servings

8 eggs
1 1/2 cups milk
1/2 cup heavy cream
1 tablespoon vanilla
1/8 teaspoon nutmeg
12 slices Italian bread, sliced 1-inch thick
1 cup crushed cornflakes
Assortment of fresh fruit (strawberries, kiwi, banana, blueberries, etc.)
Maple syrup
Powdered sugar
Whipped cream
Chopped walnuts or pecans

Preheat greased griddle.

In a large mixing bowl, whisk eggs, milk and heavy cream, about 3-4 minutes. Add vanilla and nutmeg. Dip bread into mixture. Dip one side of bread into cornflakes. Repeat with all slices.

Cook bread with cornflake-side-down first. Flip when golden brown, about 4 minutes per side. Place 2 slices on a plate and top with maple syrup, then fruit. Dust with powdered sugar. Add dollop of whipped cream and chopped nuts if desired.

Note: During the holidays, make this recipe with eggnog instead of milk and cream. This is as pretty to look at as it is to eat.

French Toast Soufflé
Serves 12

10 cups sturdy white bread, 1-inch cubed
Cooking spray
8 ounces cream cheese, softened (1/3 less fat)
8 large eggs (or 2 cups Egg Beaters)
1 1/2 cups milk (1%)
2/3 cup half-and-half
1/2 cup maple syrup
1/2 teaspoon vanilla
2 tablespoons powdered sugar
3/4 cup maple syrup

Place bread cubes in a 13 x 9-inch baking dish coated with cooking spray. Beat cream cheese at medium speed until smooth. Add eggs, one at a time, mix well after each. Add milk, half-and-half, ½ cup maple syrup, vanilla and mix until smooth. Pour cream cheese mixture over bread; cover and refrigerate overnight.

Preheat oven to 350 degrees. Bake uncovered 50 minutes or until set. To serve, sprinkle with powdered sugar and serve with warmed maple syrup.

Note: To "lighten up" this recipe, use the ingredients in parenthesis. It makes each serving 127 fewer calories, 60% less fat and a lot less cholesterol.

Orange Blossom French Toast
Serves 4

6 eggs
2/3 cup orange juice
1/3 cup Triple Sec (orange liqueur)
1/3 cup milk
1 tablespoon sugar
3 tablespoons vanilla
1/4 teaspoon salt
1/4 teaspoon cinnamon
Zest from 1 orange
8 slices French Bread, 3/4"-1" thick
Powdered sugar for garnish

Beat eggs in a large bowl. Add orange juice, Triple Sec, milk, sugar, vanilla, salt, cinnamon, and orange zest. Dip bread in egg mixture. Place single layer on a foil-lined baking sheet. Pour remaining egg mixture over the bread. Cover, refrigerate at least 1 hour or overnight so bread can soak up remaining egg. To cook, butter or spray a warmed pan or griddle. Grill 4 minutes per side (it is important not to try to cook faster, as the center of the toast will not cook). Arrange 2 slices of toast on a plate, sprinkle with powdered sugar. Garnish with seasonal fruit and a selection of syrup.

Cream Cheese French Toast with Strawberry Sauce
Makes 8 servings

Toast:
1 loaf French or sourdough bread
8 ounces cream cheese
10 eggs
1 1/2 cups half-and-half
1/4 cup maple syrup
1/4 cup butter, melted

Sauce:
2 cups fresh strawberries, sliced
2 cups strawberry preserves

Whipped cream for garnish

Grease a 11 x 7-inch baking dish. Cut enough bread to cover the bottom of the baking dish. Slice cream cheese and place over layer of bread. Cover with second layer of bread cut to cover the top.

In a mixing bowl, combine eggs, half-and-half, maple syrup and melted butter. Pour over bread layers into the baking dish; cover and refrigerate overnight.

In the morning, preheat oven to 350 degrees. Bake uncovered, 40-50 minutes or until center is set.

While baking, prepare the strawberry sauce. In a medium saucepan, combine the strawberries and preserves. Stir over medium heat until warmed.

Cut toast into 8 servings, top with strawberry sauce and garnish with whipped cream and a fanned strawberry.

Note: This is one of our most requested breakfast entrees!

Crunchy Oven French Toast
Yield: 8 slices

6 eggs
1 1/2 cups half-and-half
3 tablespoons sugar
2 teaspoons vanilla
1/4 teaspoon salt
3 cups cornflakes cereal, crushed to 1 cup
8 diagonally-cut slices French bread (3/4-inch thick)
Strawberry syrup
Fresh strawberries
Whipped cream for garnish

Grease a 15 x 10 x 1-inch baking pan. In a shallow bowl, combine eggs, half-and-half, sugar, vanilla and salt; mix well. Place crushed cereal in another shallow bowl. Soak bread in egg mixture then coat with cereal. Place in single layer in greased pan; cover. Freeze 1-2 hours or until firm.

Preheat oven to 425 degrees. Bake 15-20 minutes or until golden brown, turning once. Serve with syrup and strawberries. Garnish with whipped cream, if desired

Custard French Toast
Serves 8

8 slices French bread
1/4 cup butter, melted or softened
4 eggs
2 egg yolks
1/3 cup sugar
3 cups milk
1 cup heavy cream
1 tablespoon vanilla
1/4 teaspoon nutmeg
Powdered sugar for garnish
Fresh or canned fruit for garnish

Preheat oven to 350 degrees. Brush both sides of bread with butter. Arrange bread in an 11 x 7-inch baking pan. Beat the eggs and yolks together. Add remaining ingredients. Pour over bread. Place the French toast pan in to a larger pan. Pour enough boiling water into the outer pan to come about halfway up the side of the French toast pan. Bake 45-50 minutes or until light brown and puffy and the center is set. Let cool for 10-15 minutes before serving. Dust with powdered sugar and garnish with fresh fruits of the season.

Note: A very pretty garnish is made by using 2 slices of a peach on top with a strawberry half in the center. Arrange eight blueberries on the plate around the French toast.

Hard to Call Them Side Dishes

Sautéed Potatoes with Apple, Green Onions and Mint
Makes 6 servings

2 pounds white potatoes, peeled
4 tablespoons butter
6 green onions, finely chopped
1 small Granny Smith or Pippin apple, peeled, cored and
*   cut into 1-inch pieces*
1/4 teaspoon pepper
1 teaspoon salt
2 tablespoons finely chopped fresh mint, plus whole leaves for garnish

Boil potatoes in water, salted to taste, for 15 minutes. Drain. Cut into 1 1/2-inch pieces.

In a large nonstick frying pan over high heat, melt butter. Add potato pieces, salt and pepper. Using a spatula, turn potatoes every 5 minutes or so, sautéing until browned (about 20-25 minutes). Reduce heat to low, add green onions and apple pieces. Sauté 20 minutes more. Add chopped mint and sauté for 10 minutes.

Note: If you do not have a frying pan large enough to have the potatoes in a single layer for even browning, use two smaller pans. This is a great breakfast or dinner side dish!

Potato Gratin

Makes 8 servings

Vegetable cooking spray
1 cup chopped onion
1 clove garlic, minced
6 medium baking potatoes (about 2 1/2 pounds), cut into 1/8-inch slices
1/4 teaspoon salt
1/4 teaspoon pepper
3/4 cup shredded extra-sharp Cheddar cheese
1/4 cup grated Romano cheese
1 3/4 cup chicken broth
1 cup evaporated skimmed milk

Preheat oven to 425 degrees. Coat a 3-quart baking dish with vegetable spray.

Coat a small skillet with cooking spray; heat pan over medium heat until hot. Add onion and garlic, sauté 5 minutes until tender and set aside.

Arrange 1/3 of potato slices in prepared dish. Sprinkle with 1/8 teaspoon salt and pepper. Top with half of onion, Cheddar and Romano cheese. Repeat layers, ending with potato slices. Bring broth and milk to a boil over low heat; pour over potatoes.

Bake uncovered, 50 minutes or until tender. Let stand 5 minutes before serving.

Potato Gratin with Rosemary and Garlic

Makes 8 servings

Vegetable cooking spray
4 cloves garlic, minced
1 tablespoon fresh or 1 teaspoon dried rosemary
2 tablespoons olive oil
10-12 boiling potatoes, (about 3 1/2 pounds), cut into 1/8-inch slices
Salt and pepper to taste
1 1/2 cups chicken broth
1/2 cup shredded Parmesan cheese

Preheat oven to 400 degrees. Spray a 13 x 9-inch baking dish with vegetable spray.

Spread 1/3 potato slices in bottom of prepared dish. Sprinkle with half rosemary and garlic. Season to taste with salt and pepper. Drizzle with 1 tablespoon of oil. Repeat process for second layer using 1/2 remaining potatoes. Arrange remaining potatoes on top and pour chicken broth over all.

Bake about 1 hour and 15 minutes, until potatoes are tender, top layer is crisp and liquid is absorbed. Sprinkle with Parmesan cheese 10 minutes before ready to serve.

Gratin Dauphinois
Makes 8 servings

Butter flavored vegetable spray
6 medium red potatoes (about 2 pounds), cut into 1/8-inch slices
2 tablespoons butter, melted
1/2 teaspoon salt
1/4 teaspoon pepper
1 clove garlic, minced
1/2 cup grated Gruyere or Swiss cheese
1 cup milk

Preheat oven to 425 degrees. Coat a 11 x 7-inch baking dish with cooking spray. Arrange half of the potato slices in prepared dish. Drizzle with 1 tablespoon butter. Sprinkle with one half salt, pepper, garlic and cheese. Repeat process for second layer.

Bring milk to a boil in a small saucepan over low heat; pour over potatoes. Bake, uncovered, 45 minutes or until potatoes are tender. Let stand 10 minutes before serving.

Note: This is very quick, easy and goes with everything. To decrease calories, skim milk works just as well.

Potato-Zucchini Pancakes
Makes 6 servings

1 yellow onion, quartered
2 eggs
1 baking potato, (about 1/2 pound), peeled and cut into chunks
2 small zucchini, cut into chunks
1/2 teaspoon salt
Pinch ground pepper
2 tablespoons flour
Vegetable cooking spray

Preheat oven to 350 degrees. Line baking sheet with a double layer of paper towels.

In a food processor (using metal blade), combine onion and eggs and puree until smooth and fluffy. Add potatoes and zucchini, using on and off pulses, process until finely chopped but still with some texture. Add salt, pepper and flour, mix by hand to combine.

Spray griddle with cooking spray. Heat until test amount of batter holds together and begins to brown. Spoon tablespoons of batter onto griddle making sure pancakes do not touch. Fry until golden brown on first side, 4-5 minutes. Flip and fry 4-5 minutes longer. Transfer pancakes to towel-lined baking sheet to drain and place in oven until all are cooked. Serve immediately.

Note: Fresh pear-apple sauce or sour cream makes a nice accompaniment.

Potato Pancakes with Toasted Pecans
Makes 16 pancakes

8 medium size russet potatoes, grated
4 eggs
4 tablespoons flour
1/2 medium onion, chopped
1 teaspoon black pepper
2 teaspoons salt
1/2 teaspoon garlic, chopped
1 cup toasted pecans

Toast pecans on a cookie sheet in a 350 degree oven 10-15 minutes. Chop the pecans. Combine all ingredients except potatoes. Grate potatoes (a food processor works fine) into the mixture; mix until blended. Heat griddle to medium-hot. Spray with Pam. Ladle mixture onto hot griddle, and grill until golden on both sides.

Note: These are light and fat-free except for the eggs and the pecans. This recipe can be sized up or down—figure 1/2 potato per person.

Country French Potatoes
16 servings

3 tablespoons margarine
2 cups chopped onions
2 cups sliced mushrooms
lbs. *3 medium russet potatoes, thinly-sliced*
1 teaspoon rosemary, crushed
1 teaspoon pepper
2 teaspoons salt
2 teaspoons chicken broth mix
2 cups hot water
3 ounces Gruyere or Swiss cheese, shredded

Preheat oven to 425 degrees. Spray two 1-quart casseroles with nonstick cooking spray.

In a medium nonstick skillet, melt margarine over medium heat, add onion and mushrooms, cook over medium heat until onion is translucent, about 2 minutes. Stir in potatoes, rosemary, pepper, and salt. Transfer to prepared casserole. In a small bowl, stir together hot water and chicken broth mix. Pour over potatoes. Top evenly with cheese.

Bake uncovered, 30-35 minutes, until potatoes are fork-tender. If baked 1 hour longer, some of the liquid evaporates and the flavors intensify.

Potatoes O'Brien
Serves 16

12 baking potatoes, medium
1 medium onion, chopped
1 red bell pepper, cut in to 1-inch strips
1 green bell pepper, cut into 1-inch strips
2 teaspoons salt
1 teaspoon pepper
2 teaspoons granulated garlic
1 teaspoon paprika
5 tablespoons margarine or butter
3 tablespoons fresh parsley, chopped

Preheat oven to 350 degrees.

Bake potatoes 30 minutes. Cut potatoes into 3/4-inch cubes while still warm.

Combine all ingredients except peppers, onion and parsley in a large frying pan. Over medium heat, lightly brown potatoes. Add peppers and onions, sauté until soft.

Top with fresh chopped parsley just before serving.

Green Chili Hash Browns
16 servings

1 (32-ounce) bag frozen hash browns
2 (4-ounce) cans diced green chilies
1 (10 3/4-ounce) can cream of chicken or mushroom soup, undiluted
2 cups grated sharp Cheddar cheese, (about 8 ounces)
1 cup sour cream
Paprika for garnish

Preheat oven to 350 degrees. Grease a 13 x 9 x 2-inch glass baking dish.

Stir hash browns, green chilies, cream of chicken or cream of mushroom soup, Cheddar cheese and sour cream in a large bowl to blend. Transfer mixture to prepared baking dish.

Bake 1 1/2 hours or until crispy and browned on top.

Sprinkle with paprika and serve.

Note: Serve with Carnivore Crepes, page 38 or Cups 'O' Gold, page 28. For a moist, less crispy dish, bake about 1-1 1/4 hours.

Smoked Salmon Hash
Serves 6

2 1/2 pounds white potatoes, peeled and cut into 1/2-inch cubes
3 tablespoons butter
1 yellow onion, finely chopped
1/4 cup heavy cream
4 tablespoons fresh dill, finely chopped or 1 tablespoon dried dill
Pinch of white pepper
2 tablespoons vegetable oil
1/4 pound smoked salmon, coarsely chopped

Boil potatoes until tender, 7-10 minutes. Drain well in a colander.

Melt 1 tablespoon butter in a large frying pan over medium heat. Sauté onion until soft, 5-7 minutes.

In a large bowl, combine potatoes, sautéed onion, cream, 2 tablespoons fresh dill (or 1/2 tablespoon dried dill), 1/2 teaspoon salt and white pepper. Stir well.

Melt 2 tablespoons butter and oil in same frying pan. Add potato mixture and flatten in pan with a spatula. Cook until crust forms on underside, 7-10 minutes. Run spatula around edges to keep potatoes from sticking. Turn and continue cooking, stirring frequently, until browned, 15-20 minutes.

Add chopped salmon and mix until incorporated. Remove from heat. Garnish with remaining dill.

Note: This is wonderful with scrambled eggs or just garnished with a dollop of sour cream.

Tea-Time Sweets

Apple Brunch Cake
Serves 24

Coffee Cake:
1 cup margarine or butter, softened
1 3/4 cups sugar
1 teaspoon vanilla
4 eggs
3 cups all-purpose flour
1 1/2 teaspoons baking powder
1/2 teaspoon salt
1/4 teaspoon nutmeg
1 (21-ounce) can any fruit pie filling (apple is recommended)

Glaze:
1 1/4 cups powdered sugar
1 tablespoon margarine or butter, softened
3 teaspoons almond extract
1-2 teaspoons water

Preheat oven to 350 degrees. Grease and flour a 15 x 10 x 1-inch baking pan.

In a large bowl, combine 1 cup of margarine, sugar and vanilla. Add eggs 1 at a time, beating well after each addition. By hand, stir in flour, baking powder and salt; mix well.

Spread half of the batter in greased pan. Stir nutmeg into pie filling; spread filling evenly over batter. Drop remaining batter by teaspoonfuls over filling.

Bake 30-40 minutes or until toothpick inserted in center comes out clean and top is golden brown.

In a small bowl, blend all glaze ingredients, adding enough water for desired drizzling consistency. Drizzle over warm cake.

Pineapple Right-Side-Up Cake
Serves 12-16

Cake:
2 cups flour
1 1/2 cups sugar
1/2 cup vegetable oil
1/2 cup chopped almonds
2 eggs
1/2 teaspoon salt
1/2 teaspoon baking soda
1 teaspoon vanilla
1 (20-ounce) can crushed pineapple, drained

Icing:
*Double if using 2 round pans
8 ounces cream cheese
1/2 cup butter
1 1/2 cups confectioner's sugar
1 teaspoon vanilla
1/2 cup sliced almonds

Preheat oven to 350 degrees. Grease a 13 x 9-inch baking pan or two 8-inch round cake pans.

Combine cake ingredients in a large bowl. Beat until smooth. Pour into prepared pan(s). Bake 45 minutes (35 minutes for round pans) or until a toothpick placed in the center emerges clean. Cool before icing.

To make icing, cream together butter and cream cheese, add sugar and vanilla. Beat until smooth. Ice cake (if making a layer cake, place icing between layers and top with second cake round before icing). Sprinkle sliced almonds over top and sides.

Store in refrigerator until ready to serve.

Golden Carrot Pineapple Cake
Serves 16

Cake:
1 1/2 cups all-purpose flour
1 cup whole wheat flour
2 teaspoons baking soda
1 teaspoon cinnamon
1 teaspoon salt
1 cup sugar
2/3 cup oil
2 teaspoons vanilla
2 eggs
2 cups shredded carrots
1 (8-ounce) can crushed pineapple in its own juice, undrained
1/2 cup raisins
1/2 cup chopped nuts

Creamy Coconut Frosting
1 (8-ounce) package cream cheese, softened
2 1/2 cups powdered sugar
6 tablespoons margarine or butter, softened
2 teaspoons vanilla
1 cup coconut
1/2 cup chopped nuts

Preheat oven to 350 degrees. Grease and flour a 13 x 9-inch pan.

In a medium bowl, combine flours, baking soda, salt and cinnamon; set aside. In a large bowl, combine sugar, oil, 2 teaspoons vanilla and eggs; beat well. Stir in flour mixture; mix well. Stir in carrots, pineapple, raisins and 1/2 cup nuts. Pour batter into greased and floured pan.

Bake 30-40 minutes or until cake springs back when touched lightly in center. Cool completely.

In a small bowl, combine cream cheese, powdered sugar, margarine and 2 teaspoons vanilla; beat until smooth. Stir in coconut and 1/2 cup nuts. Spread over cooled cake.

Note: To reduce the fat in the cake, use 1/2 cup of thawed, cholesterol-free egg product for the eggs. For the frosting use 4 ounces light cream cheese, 2 tablespoons of margarine, softened, 1 cup powdered sugar and 1 teaspoon of vanilla, beat until smooth.

Heart to Heart Cheesecake

Makes 16 slices

1/3 cup graham cracker crumbs
32 ounces cream cheese, softened
1 1/3 cups sugar
4 eggs
2 tablespoons orange-flavored liqueur or orange juice
1 teaspoon grated orange peel
3 ounces semisweet chocolate, melted

Preheat oven to 325 degrees. Lightly grease bottom and sides of a 9-inch spring form pan. Sprinkle graham cracker crumbs over bottom and sides of pan.

In a large bowl, beat cream cheese until smooth. Gradually add sugar, beating until smooth. At low speed, add eggs 1 at a time, beating until blended. Add liqueur and orange peel; beat 2 minutes, scraping sides of bowl.

In a small bowl, reserve 1 cup of batter. Pour remaining batter into crumb-lined pan.

Blend melted chocolate into reserved batter. Spoon chocolate batter by teaspoonfuls onto batter in pan, forming a circle of nine drops around the outside and five drops in the center. Continue to spoon batter onto drops using all of chocolate batter. Starting in the center of an outer drop, run knife through the centers of outer drops forming a connection ring; repeat with center drops.

Bake about 1 hour. Center should jiggle slightly. Turn off oven and let cake cool for 1 hour in the oven. Remove sides of pan and refrigerate.

Note: Place a pan of boiling hot water on the shelf below the cheesecake during baking. The moisture and slow cool down in the oven will help prevent cracking.

Almond Tea Cake

Cake:
2/3 cup brown sugar
2/3 cup sugar
2/3 cup vegetable oil
1/2 teaspoon salt
2 large eggs
1 cup buttermilk
1 1/4 cups flour
1/2 teaspoon baking soda
1/2 teaspoon baking powder
1/2 teaspoon almond extract
Sliced almonds

Glaze:
1/2 cup powdered sugar
2 tablespoons water
1/2 teaspoon vanilla

Preheat oven to 350 degrees. Grease a 13 x 9-inch baking pan.

Mix sugars, oil and salt together until smooth. Add eggs and 1/2 cup buttermilk. In a separate bowl, mix the flour, baking soda, and baking powder. Stir into the sugar mixture. Add another 1/2 cup buttermilk and almond extract.

Pour into prepared pan. Sprinkle with sliced almonds.

Bake 30-40 minutes, until golden brown. Do not overbake; it should be moist.

Make glaze by combining all glaze ingredients. Brush over cake while still hot. To serve, cut away edges, as they tend to be dry.

Raspberry Cream Cheese Coffee Cake
Yield: 16 servings

2 1/4 cups all-purpose flour
3/4 cup sugar
3/4 cup margarine or butter
1/2 teaspoon baking powder
1/2 teaspoon baking soda
1/4 teaspoon salt
3/4 cup dairy sour cream
1 teaspoon almond extract
1 egg

1 (8-ounce) package cream cheese, softened
1/4 cup sugar
1 egg
1/2 cup raspberry preserves
1/2 cup sliced almonds

Preheat oven to 350 degrees. Grease and flour bottom and sides of a 9 or 10-inch spring form pan.

In a large bowl, combine flour and 3/4 cup sugar. Using pastry blender or fork, cut in margarine until mixture resembles coarse crumbs. Reserve 1 cup of crumb mixture. To remaining crumb mixture, add baking powder, baking soda, salt, sour cream, almond extract and 1 egg; blend well. Spread batter over bottom and 2 inches up sides of greased and floured pan. (Batter should be about 1/4-inch thick on sides.)

In a small bowl, combine cream cheese, 1/4 cup sugar and 1 egg; blend well. Pour into batter-lined pan. Carefully spoon preserves evenly over cream cheese mixture.

In a small bowl, combine reserved crumb mixture and sliced almonds. Sprinkle over preserves.

Bake 45-55 minutes or until cream cheese filling is set and crust is deep golden brown. Cool 15 minutes. Remove sides of pan. Serve warm or cool, cut into wedges. Store in refrigerator.

Note: Easy to make yet impressive to serve!

Ultimate Apple Streusel Coffee Cake
Serves 8

Coffee Cake:
1/2 cup sugar
2 eggs
1 1/2 teaspoons grated lemon peel
1/2 cup vanilla yogurt
3 tablespoons butter or margarine, melted
1 1/3 cups all-purpose flour
2 teaspoons baking powder
1/2 teaspoon salt
2 Granny Smith apples, peeled and chopped
1 Granny Smith apple, peeled and thinly sliced

Streusel Topping:
2/3 cup all-purpose flour
1 cup firmly packed brown sugar
1 teaspoon cinnamon
1/2 cup butter or margarine, softened
1/2 cup chopped walnuts

Glaze:
1 cup powdered sugar
1 tablespoon butter or margarine, softened
1 1/2 teaspoons almond extract
2-3 teaspoons water

Preheat oven to 350 degrees. Grease a 10-inch tart or 9-inch spring form pan.

In a medium bowl, beat 1/2 cup sugar and 2 eggs; stir in lemon peel, yogurt and 3 tablespoons butter. Add flour, baking powder and salt to egg mixture; blend well. Stir in 2 chopped apples. Pour into greased pan. Arrange the remaining sliced apple on top of dough, overlapping slightly.

In a medium bowl, combine 2/3 cup flour, brown sugar, and cinnamon. Using pastry blender or fork cut in 1/2 cup butter until mixture is crumbly. Spread mixture over the sliced apples.

Bake 35-45 minutes or until toothpick inserted in center comes out clean.

Meanwhile, in a small bowl combine all glaze ingredients and blend well. Drizzle over warm cake. Store in refrigerator.

Winter Fruit Coffee Cake
Makes 8-10 servings

Coffee Cake:
1 1/2 cups all-purpose flour
2 teaspoons baking powder
3/4 cup sugar
1/4 cup margarine or butter, softened
2 eggs
1/2 cup buttermilk
2 teaspoons grated orange peel
1/2 cup raisins
1 cup thinly sliced apples
1 orange, peeled, thinly sliced

Topping:
1/4 cup sugar
1/2 teaspoon cinnamon
2 tablespoons margarine or butter, melted
1/2 cup chopped pecans

Preheat oven to 350 degrees. Grease and flour a 9-inch spring form pan.

In a medium bowl, combine flour and baking powder; set aside. In a large bowl, beat 3/4 cup sugar and 1/4 cup margarine until light and fluffy. Add eggs; blend well. Alternately add dry ingredients and buttermilk to sugar mixture, beating well after each addition. Stir in orange peel and raisins. Pour into greased pan. Arrange apple and orange slices decoratively over top of batter.

In a small bowl, combine all topping ingredients; arrange over fruit in a pinwheel.

Bake 40-50 minutes or until golden brown. Cool 10 minutes; remove sides of pan.

Note: To serve, top with whipped cream or serve warm from the oven garnished with orange curls and apple slices.

Sleep-Over Coffee Cake
Serves 8-10

Cake:
2 cups flour
1 cup sugar
1 cup buttermilk
2/3 cup butter, softened
1/2 cup packed brown sugar
2 large eggs
2 tablespoons dry milk powder
1 tablespoon cinnamon
1 teaspoon baking soda
1 teaspoon baking powder
1/2 teaspoon salt

Topping:
1/2 cup packed brown sugar
1/2 cup walnuts or pecans, chopped
1/2 teaspoon ground nutmeg
1/4 cup butter, melted

Grease and flour a 13 x 9-inch baking pan.

In a large bowl of an electric mixer, combine all cake ingredients. Mix at low speed until well-blended, about 4 minutes. Place in prepared pan.

Mix dry topping ingredients together and sprinkle evenly over the batter. Cover and refrigerate overnight.

Preheat oven to 350 degrees.

Remove cake from refrigerator. Drizzle with melted butter. Bake 30 minutes, until top is a rich golden brown. Cool for 15 minutes and serve warm.

Note: This is a real time saver when entertaining house guests. Your guests will awaken to the aroma of freshly baked pastry. What could be more inviting?

Blueberry Buckle Ring
Makes 12 servings

Cake:
1 1/2 cups flour
2 teaspoons baking powder
1/4 teaspoon salt
3/4 cup sugar
1/4 cup margarine or butter, softened
1 egg
1/2 cup milk
3 cups fresh or frozen, unthawed blueberries

Topping:
1/3 cup all-purpose flour
1/2 cup firmly packed brown sugar
1/2 teaspoon cinnamon
1/4 cup margarine or butter
1/4 cup chopped walnuts

Preheat oven to 350 degrees. Grease and flour a 10-inch tube or spring form pan.

In a medium bowl, combine 1 1/2 cups flour, baking powder and salt: set aside. In a large bowl, beat sugar and 1/4 cup butter until light and fluffy. Add egg and beat well. Alternately add dry ingredients and milk to sugar mixture, beating well after each addition.

Spread 2/3 of batter into greased pan and top with blueberries. Carefully spread with remaining batter.

In a medium bowl, combine 1/3 cup flour, brown sugar, and cinnamon. Using pastry blender or fork, cut in 1/4 cup butter until mixture is crumbly. Stir in nuts and sprinkle mixture over batter.

Bake 55-65 minutes or until cake is golden brown. Cool 10 minutes. Remove from pan. Serve warm or cooled.

Persimmon Cream Tart
Serves 8-10

Crust:
1 1/3 cups flour
1/4 cup sugar
1/2 cup butter, cut into chunks
1 large egg yolk

Filling:
16 ounces cream cheese, at room temperature
1/2 cup orange marmalade
3 fuyu persimmons (3/4 pound total)

Preheat oven to 350 degrees.

Crust: In a bowl, combine flour and sugar. Add butter; mix until fine crumbs form. Add egg yolk; mix with a fork until dough sticks together. Pat into a ball. Press dough over bottom and up sides, flush with rim, of a 10-10 1/2-inch tart pan with removable rim. Bake 35-40 minutes until golden brown; let cool.

Filling: In a small bowl, beat cream cheese and 6 tablespoons marmalade until well blended. Spoon into cooled crust and spread evenly.

Rinse, stem and peel persimmons then cut lengthwise into 1/4-inch wedges; discard seeds. Lay fruit in concentric circles on filling, overlap slightly.

Heat remaining marmalade in a glass measuring cup in a microwave until melted. Gently brush melted marmalade over persimmon slices.

Remove pan rim and cut. Keep refrigerated until serving.

Note: I never knew what to do with persimmons until a guest gave me a shopping bag full. This is as good as it is easy to make!

Raspberry and Pear Tart
Makes 8 servings

Crust:
1/4 cup margarine or butter, softened
2 tablespoons sugar
Dash of salt
1/2 teaspoon grated lemon peel
1.2 teaspoon vanilla
1 egg yolk
3/4 cup all-purpose flour
1/4 cup finely ground blanched almonds

Filling:
4 tablespoons red raspberry jelly
1/2 cup all-purpose flour
3 tablespoons sugar
1/4 cup margarine or butter, softened
1/2 teaspoon grated lemon peel
1/2 teaspoon almond extract
1 (3-ounce) package cream cheese, softened
1 egg
5 canned pear halves, well drained
1 cup fresh or frozen raspberries or strawberries, slightly thawed

Preheat oven to 350 degrees.

In a small bowl, combine 1/4 cup margarine, 2 tablespoons sugar and salt; beat at medium speed until light and fluffy. Add 1/2 teaspoon lemon peel, vanilla and egg yolk; beat until smooth. Stir in 3/4 cup flour and almonds; blend well. Press mixture in bottom and up sides of a 10-inch tart pan or a 9-inch spring form pan. Bake 10 minutes; cool.

Brush baked crust with 2 tablespoons of the jelly. In a small bowl, combine 1/2 cup flour, 3 tablespoons sugar, 1/4 cup margarine, 1/2 teaspoon grated lemon peel, almond extract, cream cheese and egg; beat 1 minute at medium speed. Pour filling over crust. Arrange pear halves on filling, rounded sides up and narrow ends pointing toward center.

Bake 25-35 minutes or until center is set.

In small saucepan, heat 2 tablespoons jelly until melted. Arrange berries in rows between pear halves. Brush jelly over pears, berries and filling.

Sunburst Lemon Bars
Makes 24 bars

Crust:
2 cups all-purpose flour
1/2 cup powdered sugar
1 cup margarine or butter, softened

Filling:
4 eggs, slightly beaten
2 cups sugar
1/4 cup all-purpose flour
1 teaspoon baking powder
1/4 cup lemon juice

Frosting:
1 cup powdered sugar
2-3 tablespoons lemon juice

Preheat oven to 350 degrees.

In a large bowl, combine all crust ingredients at low speed until crumbly. Press mixture evenly in bottom of an ungreased 13 x 9-inch pan.

Bake 20-30 minutes or until light golden brown.

Meanwhile, in a large bowl combine all filling ingredients except lemon juice; blend well. Stir in 1/4 cup lemon juice. Pour mixture over warm crust. Return to oven and bake an additional 25-30 minutes or until top is light golden brown. Cool completely.

In a small bowl, combine 1 cup powdered sugar and enough lemon juice for desired spreading consistency; blend until smooth. Spread over cooled cake. Cut into bars.

Note: Guests rave about this every time we serve it. For a pretty presentation, cut off edges, sprinkle with powdered sugar and lemon zest.

Pumpkin Bars
Makes 24 bars

Bars:
2 cups all-purpose flour
2 cups sugar
2 teaspoons baking powder
1 teaspoon baking soda
1 teaspoon cinnamon
1 teaspoon nutmeg
1/2 teaspoon salt
1/2 teaspoon cloves
1 cup oil
2 cups pumpkin
4 eggs
1/2 cup chopped nuts
1/2 cup raisins

Frosting:
2 cups powdered sugar
1/3 cup margarine or butter, softened
1 (3-ounce) package cream cheese, softened
1 tablespoon milk
1 teaspoon vanilla

Preheat oven to 350 degrees. Grease a 13 x 9-inch baking pan.

In a large bowl, combine all bar ingredients except nuts and raisins; beat at low speed until moistened. Beat 2 minutes at medium speed. Stir in nuts and raisins. Pour into greased pan.

Bake 35-45 minutes or until toothpick inserted in center comes out clean. Cool completely.

In a small bowl, combine all frosting ingredients; beat until smooth. Frost cooled cake. Cut into bars. Store in refrigerator.

Oatmeal Carmelitas
Makes 24 bars

Crust:
2 cups flour
2 cups rolled oats
1 1/2 cups packed brown sugar
1 teaspoon baking soda
1/2 teaspoon salt
1 1/4 cups margarine or butter, softened

Filling:
1 cup caramel ice cream topping
3 tablespoons flour
1 cup semisweet chocolate chips
1/2 cup chopped nuts

Preheat oven to 350 degrees. Grease a 13 x 9-inch pan.

In a large bowl, combine all crust ingredients and mix at low speed until crumbly. Reserve half of crumb mixture (about 3 cups) for topping. Press remaining crumb mixture in bottom of greased pan. Bake for 10 minutes.

Meanwhile, in a small bowl, combine caramel topping and 3 tablespoons flour.

Remove partially baked base from oven; sprinkle with chocolate chips and nuts. Drizzle evenly with caramel mixture; sprinkle with reserved crumb mixture.

Bake an additional 18-22 minutes or until golden brown. Cool completely. Refrigerate 1-2 hours or until filling is set. Cut into bars.

English Matrimonials
Makes 12 squares

1 1/4 cups flour
1 cup packed brown sugar
1 1/2 cups oatmeal
1/2 teaspoon salt
3/4 cup butter, melted
3/4 cup raspberry jam
1 teaspoon almond extract

Preheat oven to 325 degrees. Lightly grease an 8-inch square pan.

Combine all ingredients except jam and almond extract. Pat half of mixture into prepared pan. Mix jam and almond extract. Spread over oat mixture. Pat other half of oat mixture on top.

Bake 40-45 minutes or until light golden brown. Cut into 1-inch bars when cool.

Note: A quick and easy dessert that appeals to adults and children.

Praline Cheesecake Bars
Makes 24 bars

3/4 cup butter, softened
1 cup sugar, divided
1 teaspoon vanilla, divided
1 1/2 cups flour
16 ounces cream cheese, softened
2 eggs
1/2 cup almond brickle (toffee) chips
3 tablespoons caramel ice cream topping

Preheat oven to 350 degrees.

Mix butter, 1/2 cup sugar and 1/2 teaspoon vanilla on medium speed until light and fluffy. Gradually add flour, mixing on low speed until blended. Press into bottom of a 13 x 9-inch baking pan.

Bake 20-23 minutes or until lightly browned. Cool.

Mix cream cheese, remaining 1/2 cup sugar and 1/2 teaspoon vanilla on medium speed until blended. Add eggs; mix well. Blend in chips. Spread over crust. Drizzle caramel topping over cream cheese mixture. Cut through batter with butter knife to marbleize the batter.

Bake 30 minutes. Cool on wire rack then refrigerate until serving.

Coconut Mud Bars
Makes 24 bars

Bottom layer:
1 1/3 cups flour
1/2 teaspoon baking powder
Pinch of salt
1/2 cup packed brown sugar
1/2 cup butter, slightly softened and cut into small pieces

Ganache:
10 ounces semisweet chocolate, chopped
3/4 cup heavy cream

Topping:
1/4 cup butter, softened
1/2 cup granulated sugar
2 teaspoons vanilla extract
1/4 teaspoon coconut extract (optional)
2 large eggs
1 1/2 cups shredded coconut
1 1/2 cups chopped pecans

Preheat oven to 350 degrees. Lightly grease a 13 x 9-inch pan.

Make the bottom layer: In a medium bowl, whisk together the flour, baking powder, salt and brown sugar. With a pastry blender, cut the butter into the dry ingredients until mixture resembles coarse meal. Press mixture into the bottom of prepared pan. Bake 10 minutes, or until crust is just set. Place on a rack to cool, but leave the oven on.

Meanwhile, make the ganache: Place chocolate in a medium bowl. In a small saucepan, bring the cream to a simmer. Pour hot cream over the chocolate; let stand for 5 minutes, then stir until smooth. Pour the ganache over the crust and refrigerate about 15 minutes to set the ganache.

Prepare the topping: In a medium bowl, cream the butter. Add sugar, vanilla and coconut extract (optional) and beat until blended. Beat in the eggs. Stir in coconut and pecans.

Drop the coconut-pecan topping evenly over the ganache and spread gently.

Bake 25-30 minutes, or until the top is golden brown. Set on a wire rack to cool. Cut into bars.

Sour Cream Apple Squares

Makes 16 squares

Squares:
2 cups all-purpose flour
2 cups firmly packed brown sugar
1/2 cup margarine or butter, softened
1 cup chopped nuts
1-2 teaspoons cinnamon
1 teaspoon baking soda
1/2 teaspoon salt
1 cup dairy sour cream
1 teaspoon vanilla
1 egg
2 cups finely chopped peeled apples

Preheat oven to 350 degrees.

In a large bowl, combine flour, brown sugar and margarine; beat at low speed until crumbly. Stir in nuts. Press 2 3/4 cups of crumb mixture in bottom of an ungreased 13 x 9-inch pan.

To the remaining mixture, add cinnamon, baking soda, salt, sour cream, vanilla and egg; mix well. Stir in apples. Spoon evenly over base.

Bake 30-40 minutes or until toothpick inserted in center comes out clean. Cut into squares.

Serve with whipped cream or ice cream, if desired. Can also be topped with a streusel topping before baking.

Streusel Topping:
¾ cup flour
½ cup firmly packed brown sugar
½ teaspoon cinnamon
1/3 cup butter

In a medium bowl, combine topping ingredients until crumbly; sprinkle over filling.

mmm . . . Chocolate!

Chocolate Chip Cheesecake
Makes 10-16 servings

Crust:
2 cups crushed crème-filled chocolate sandwich cookies (20 cookies)
2 tablespoons margarine or butter, melted

Filling:
3 eggs
2 (8-ounce) packages cream cheese, softened
3/4 cup sugar
1 teaspoon vanilla
1/2 cup whipping cream
1 cup miniature semisweet chocolate chips

Glaze:
1/4 cup miniature semisweet chocolate chips
1 teaspoon shortening

Preheat oven to 325 degrees.

In a medium bowl, combine crust ingredients; press in bottom and 1 inch up the sides of an ungreased 10-inch spring form pan.

Beat eggs in a large bowl. Add cream cheese, sugar and vanilla; beat until smooth. Add whipping cream; blend well. Stir in 1 cup chocolate chips. Pour into crust-lined pan. Bake 60-75 minutes or until center is set. Cool.

In a small saucepan over low heat, melt glaze ingredients, stirring constantly. Drizzle over cooled cheesecake. Refrigerate several hours or overnight. Carefully remove sides of pan before serving.

Note: To help prevent cracking of the cheesecake, place a pan of boiling water on the oven rack below the cheesecake. Also, bake until center is slightly underdone, turn off oven and let the cheesecake cool slowly in the oven.

Chocolate Chip Zucchini Cake
Serves 16

Cake:
1 1/2 cups sugar
1/2 cup margarine or butter, softened
1/4 cup oil
1 teaspoon vanilla
2 eggs
2 1/2 cups all-purpose flour
¼ cup unsweetened cocoa
1 teaspoon baking soda
1/2 cup buttermilk
2 cups shredded zucchini
1/2-1 cup semisweet chocolate chips
1/2 cup chopped nuts

Frosting:
2/3 cup butter, softened
4 cups powdered sugar
1 teaspoon vanilla
1/3 cup unsweetened cocoa
4-6 tablespoons half-and-half
Chocolate shots

Preheat oven to 350 degrees. Grease and flour a 13 x 9-inch pan.

In a large bowl, combine sugar, margarine, oil, vanilla, and eggs; beat well. Add flour, cocoa, baking soda and buttermilk; blend well. Fold in zucchini, chocolate chips and nuts. Spread in prepared pan.

Bake 35-45 minutes or until toothpick inserted in center comes out clean. Cool completely.

For frosting, beat butter until light and fluffy. Gradually add powdered sugar. Beat in vanilla and half-and-half (adding enough for desired spreading consistency). Frost cake and sprinkle with chocolate shots.

Chocolate Sour Cream Cake

Makes 12 servings

Cake:
2 cups flour
2 cups sugar
1 1/4 teaspoons baking soda
1 teaspoon salt
1/2 teaspoon baking powder
1 cup water
3/4 cup dairy sour cream
1/4 cup shortening
1 teaspoon vanilla
2 eggs
4 ounces unsweetened chocolate, melted and cooled

Sour Cream Chocolate Frosting:
3 cups powdered sugar
1/4 cup dairy sour cream
1/4 cup margarine or butter, softened
3 tablespoons milk
1 teaspoon vanilla
3 ounces unsweetened chocolate, melted and cooled

Preheat oven to 350 degrees. Grease and flour two 8 or 9-inch round cake pans; line bottom of pans with waxed paper.

In a medium bowl, combine flour, sugar, baking soda, salt and baking powder; blend well. In a large bowl, combine remaining cake ingredients; add dry ingredients. Blend at low speed until moistened; beat 3 minutes at high speed. Pour batter into greased, floured and lined pans.

Bake 30-40 minutes or until toothpick inserted in center comes out clean. Cool 10 minutes; remove from pans. Cool completely.

In a small bowl, combine all frosting ingredients at low speed until moistened, beat at high speed until smooth and creamy. To assemble cake, place 1 cake layer, top side down, on serving plate; spread evenly with about 1/4 of frosting. Top with remaining cake layer, top side up. Spread sides and top of cake with remaining frosting.

White Chocolate Almond Bars
Makes 16 bars

2 ounces white baking bar, chopped
1/2 cup margarine or butter
3/4 cup sugar
2 eggs
1 teaspoon almond extract
2/3 cup all-purpose flour
1/2 teaspoon baking powder
1/4 teaspoon salt
1/2 cup chopped almonds
1 tablespoon powdered sugar
1/2 cup sliced almonds

Preheat oven to 350 degrees. Grease and lightly flour bottom only of a 9-inch square pan.

Melt white baking bar in medium saucepan over very low heat, stirring constantly until smooth. Add margarine; stir until melted. Remove from heat; stir in sugar. Beat in eggs 1 at a time. Add almond extract. Add flour, baking powder, salt and almonds to chocolate mixture; mix well. Spread in prepared pan. Sprinkle liberally with almonds. Bake 25-35 minutes or until golden brown and center is set. Cool completely. Sprinkled with powdered sugar. Cut into bars.

Chocolate Macadamia Cookies with White Chocolate Chips
Makes about 3 dozen

3/4 cup packed brown sugar
1/2 cup sugar
1 cup butter, softened
1 teaspoon almond extract
1 egg
2 cups flour
1/4 cup unsweetened cocoa
1 teaspoon baking soda
1/2 teaspoon salt
1 cup white chocolate chips
4 ounces macadamia nuts, coarsely chopped

Preheat oven to 350 degrees.

In a large bowl, combine sugars and butter, beat until light and fluffy. Add almond extract and egg; blend well. Add flour, cocoa, baking soda and salt; mix well. Stir in white chocolate chips and nuts. Drop by rounded tablespoonfuls onto ungreased cookie sheet. Bake 10-13 minutes or until set. Cool 1 minute, remove from cookie sheet.

Ultimate Chocolate Chocolate Cookies

Make 1 1/2 dozen cookies

16 ounces semisweet baking chocolate, divided
3/4 cup packed brown sugar
1/4 cup butter
2 eggs
1 teaspoon vanilla
1/2 cup flour
1/4 teaspoon baking powder
2 cups chopped nuts (optional)

Coarsely chop 8 ounces chocolate, set aside. Melt remaining 8 ounces chocolate with butter until smooth. Stir in sugar, eggs and vanilla. Stir in flour and baking powder. Stir in chopped chocolate and nuts. Refrigerate 1-2 hours for easier handling. Preheat oven to 350 degrees. Drop dough by ample tablespoonfuls onto ungreased cookie sheet. Bake 13 minutes or until cookie is puffed and feels set to touch. Cool on cookie sheet 1 minute before removing to wire rack to cool.

Note: The dough has a very sticky, frosting like consistency—don't be fooled, the cookies are decadent.

Raspberry Fudge Brownies

Makes 16 bars

1/2 cup butter
3 ounces bittersweet chocolate
*   or 1 ounce unsweetened and 2 ounces semisweet chocolate*
1 cup sugar
2 eggs
1 teaspoon vanilla
3/4 cup flour
1/4 teaspoon baking powder
Dash of salt
1/2 cup sliced almonds
1/2 cup raspberry preserves
1 cup chocolate chips

Preheat oven to 350 degrees. Grease an 8-inch square pan. Melt butter and bittersweet chocolate in saucepan over low heat. Remove from heat; cool. Beat sugar, eggs and vanilla in a large bowl until light. Beat in chocolate mixture. Stir in flour, baking powder and salt until just blended. Spread 3/4 batter in prepared pan; sprinkle almonds over top. Bake 10 minutes. Remove from oven; spread preserves over almonds. Carefully spoon remaining batter over preserves, smoothing top. Bake 30 minutes or until top feels firm. Remove from oven; sprinkle chocolate chips over top. Let stand several minutes until chips melt, spread evenly over brownies. Cool completely in pan. Place in refrigerator until set; cut into squares.

Twice-Topped Brownies
Makes 16 bars

Brownies:
4 ounces unsweetened chocolate
1/2 cup butter
3/4 cup flour
1/4 teaspoon salt
2 eggs
1 cup packed brown sugar
2 teaspoons vanilla
1/2 cup chopped pecans
1/2 cup mini chocolate chips

Vanilla Cream:
1/2 cup butter
4 ounces cream cheese, softened
1 teaspoon vanilla
1 1/4 cups powdered sugar

Chocolate Drizzle:
2 ounces semisweet chocolate chips
2 tablespoons heavy cream

Preheat oven to 350 degrees. Grease an 11 x 7-inch baking pan.

In a double broiler, melt unsweetened chocolate and butter together, stirring until smooth. Set aside to cool slightly.

In a small bowl, whisk together flour and salt. In a medium bowl, beat eggs and brown sugar. Beat in chocolate mixture and vanilla. Stir in flour mixture. Stir in pecans and mini chocolate chips.

Spread batter in prepared pan. Bake 22-25 minutes. Cool in pan on a rack.

In a medium bowl, cream butter and cream cheese until light and fluffy. Gradually beat in vanilla and powdered sugar. Spread over cooled brownies. Refrigerate until set.

In a double broiler, melt chocolate chips and cream. Stir until smooth, then set aside to cool slightly. Drizzle melted chocolate randomly over vanilla cream layer. Chill until ready to serve.

Marbleized Mint Brownies
Makes 24 bars

Filling:
1 (8-ounce) package cream cheese, softened
1/4 cup sugar
1 egg
1 teaspoon mint extract
4 drops green food coloring

Brownies:
1 cup butter
4 ounces unsweetened chocolate (cut into pieces)
2 cups sugar
2 teaspoons vanilla
4 eggs
1 cup flour

Frosting:
2 tablespoons margarine or butter
2 tablespoons corn syrup
2 tablespoons water
2 ounces unsweetened chocolate cut into pieces
1 teaspoon vanilla
1 cup powdered sugar

Preheat oven to 350 degrees. Grease and flour a 13 x 9-inch pan.

In a small bowl, beat cream cheese and 1/4 cup sugar until smooth. Add 1 egg, mint extract and food coloring; mix well and set aside.

In large saucepan, melt 1 cup butter and 4 ounces chocolate over very low heat, stirring constantly. Remove from heat; cool slightly. Stir in 2 cups sugar and 2 teaspoons vanilla. Add 4 eggs, 1 at a time, beating well after each addition. Stir in flour; mix well. Spread in greased and floured pan.

Carefully spoon filling over brownie mixture. Lightly swirl filling into brownie mixture.

Bake 45-50 minutes or until set. Cool completely.

In a heavy saucepan, bring 2 tablespoons margarine, corn syrup and water to a rolling boil. Remove from heat. Add 2 ounces chocolate; stir until melted. Stir in 1 teaspoon vanilla and powdered sugar; beat until smooth. Frost cooled brownie mixture. Cut into bars. Store in refrigerator.

mmm . . . Chocolate!

Raspberry Cream Brownie Wedges
Makes 12 servings

Filling:
1 (8-ounce) package cream cheese, softened
1/2 cup raspberry preserves
1 tablespoon all-purpose flour
1 egg
2-3 drops red food coloring

Brownie:
3/4 cup margarine or butter
4 ounces unsweetened chocolate
3/4 cup sugar
3 eggs
1 cup all-purpose flour
1/2 teaspoon baking powder
1/4 teaspoon salt
3 tablespoons raspberry-flavored liqueur or water

Glaze:
1 ounce white baking bar
2 teaspoons oil

Preheat oven to 350 degrees. Lightly grease a 9-inch spring form pan.

In a small bowl, combine all filling ingredients. Beat 1 minute at medium speed; set aside.

In medium saucepan, melt margarine and chocolate over low heat, stirring constantly. Remove from heat; cool slightly. Add sugar and 3 eggs; beat well. Stir in flour, baking powder and salt; blend well. Stir in raspberry liqueur.

Spread half of chocolate mixture in bottom of greased pan. Spread filling evenly over chocolate. Spread remaining chocolate mixture evenly over filling.

Bake 37-42 minutes or until center is set. Cool on wire rack 5 minutes; run knife around edge of pan to loosen. Cool completely; remove from pan.

In small saucepan, melt glaze ingredients over low heat, stirring constantly until smooth. Drizzle glaze over top of brownie; allow to set. Cut into wedges.

"I Want Cookie!"

Hugs and Kisses Cookies
Makes 3 dozen

2 3/4 cups flour
1 1/2 teaspoons baking soda
1 1/2 teaspoons salt
1 cup butter, softened not melted
1 1/2 cups brown sugar
2 eggs
4 tablespoons milk
2 teaspoons vanilla
3 cups oatmeal
2 cups chopped nuts
Hershey Kisses with Almonds

Preheat oven to 350 degrees.

Mix together flour, soda and salt. Add butter, sugar, eggs, milk and vanilla. Mix until smooth. Blend in oatmeal and nuts. Drop spoonfuls onto greased cookie sheet.

Bake 12-14 minutes. While cookies are baking unwrap Hershey Kisses. Top each cookie with a kiss as soon as they are removed from the oven. Place in refrigerator for a few minutes to firm up chocolate.

Note: We mix all of our cookie dough by hand so that they do not have a "homogenized, store-bought" consistency.

Peanut Blossoms
Makes 4 dozen

1 3/4 cups all-purpose flour
1/2 cup sugar
1/2 cup firmly packed brown sugar
1 teaspoon baking soda
1/2 teaspoon salt
1/2 cup shortening
1/2 cup peanut butter
2 tablespoons milk
1 teaspoon vanilla
1 egg
Granulated sugar
48 Hershey's Kisses

Preheat oven to 350 degrees.

In a large bowl, combine flour, 1/2 cup sugar, brown sugar, baking soda, salt, shortening, peanut butter, milk, vanilla and egg; blend at low speed until a stiff dough forms. Shape into 1-inch balls; roll in sugar. Place 2 inches apart on ungreased cookie sheets.

Bake 10-12 minutes or until golden brown. Immediately top each cookie with a candy kiss, pressing down firmly so cookie cracks around edge; remove from cookie sheets. Cool completely. Place in the refrigerator to firm up the chocolate quickly.

Crisp Chocolate Snaps
Makes 5 dozen

2 cups sugar
1 cup packed brown sugar
1 1/2 cups butter, softened
6 ounces unsweetened chocolate, melted, cooled
2 teaspoons vanilla
1/2 teaspoon red food coloring, optional
3 eggs
4 cups flour
2 teaspoons baking soda
1 teaspoon salt
1/4 cup granulated sugar

In a large bowl, combine 2 cups sugar, brown sugar and butter; beat until light and fluffy. Add chocolate, vanilla, food color and eggs; blend well. Add flour, baking soda and salt; mix well. Refrigerate 1-2 hours for easier handling.
Preheat oven to 350 degrees. Lightly grease cookie sheet. Shape dough into 1 1/2-inch balls. Roll in sugar. Bake 10-12 minutes. Cool 1 minute, remove from cookie sheets.

Note: The red food coloring gives these cookies the look of devil's food cake.

Pumpkin Cookies with Penuche Frosting
Makes 4 dozen

Cookies:
1/2 cup sugar
1/2 cup packed brown sugar
1 cup butter
1 cup canned pumpkin
1 teaspoon vanilla
1 egg
2 cups flour
1 teaspoon baking powder
1 teaspoon baking soda
1 teaspoon cinnamon
1/4 teaspoon salt
3/4 cup chopped walnuts or pecans

Penuche Frosting:
3 tablespoons margarine or butter
1/2 cup packed brown sugar
1/4 cup milk
1 1/2-2 cups powdered sugar

Preheat oven to 350 degrees.

In a large bowl, beat sugar, 1/2 cup brown sugar and 1 cup butter until light and fluffy. Add pumpkin, vanilla and egg; blend well. Add flour, baking powder, baking soda, cinnamon and salt; mix well. Stir in nuts.

Drop dough by rounded teaspoonfuls 2 inches apart onto ungreased cookie sheets. Bake 10-12 minutes or until light golden brown around edges. Immediately remove from cookie sheets. Cool completely.

In medium saucepan, combine 3 tablespoons margarine and 1/2 cup brown sugar. Bring to a boil. Cook over medium heat 1 minute or until slightly thickened, stirring constantly. Cool 10 minutes. Add milk; beat until smooth. Beat in enough powdered sugar for desired spreading consistency. Frost cooled cookies; place in refrigerator to set frosting.

Oatmeal Scotchies

Makes 3-4 dozen cookies

> 3/4 cup butter, softened
> 3/4 cup granulated sugar
> 3/4 cup packed brown sugar
> 2 eggs
> 1 teaspoon vanilla
> 1 1/4 cups flour
> 1 teaspoon baking soda
> 1/2 teaspoon cinnamon
> 1/2 teaspoon salt
> 3 cups rolled oats
> 10-ounce package butterscotch chips

Preheat oven to 350 degrees.

In a large bowl, beat butter and sugars until well blended. Add eggs and vanilla; blend thoroughly. Stir together flour, soda, cinnamon and salt; gradually add to butter mixture, beat until well blended. Stir in oats and butterscotch chips.

Drop by tablespoonfuls onto ungreased cookie sheet. Bake 11-13 minutes. Cool slightly before removing to wire rack to cool completely.

Chocolate Almond Bonbons

Makes 4 dozen cookies

> 4 ounces German baking chocolate
> 2 tablespoons milk
> 1/4 cup sugar
> 3/4 cup butter, softened
> 2 teaspoons vanilla
> 2 cups flour
> 1/4 teaspoon salt
> 3 1/2-ounce tube almond paste
> Granulated sugar for rolling

Preheat oven to 350 degrees.

In a small saucepan over low heat, melt chocolate in milk until smooth, stirring occasionally. In a large bowl, beat 1/4 cup sugar and butter until fluffy. Blend in chocolate and vanilla. Stir in flour and salt; mix well.

Using rounded teaspoonfuls of dough, shape into balls. Make an indentation in center of each cookie; fill with scant 1/4 teaspoon almond paste. Press dough around filling to cover. Bake 11-13 minutes until set. Remove and roll in sugar. Cool completely.

Raspberry Almond Shortbread Thumb Print Cookies
Makes 3 dozen cookies

Cookies:
2/3 cup sugar
1 cup butter, softened
1/2 teaspoon almond extract
2 cups all-purpose flour
1/2 cup raspberry jam
Pecans

Glaze:
1 cup powdered sugar
1 1/2 teaspoons almond extract
2-3 teaspoons water

In a large mixing bowl combine sugar, butter and almond extract. Beat at medium speed until creamy (2-3 minutes). Reduce speed to low; add flour. Beat until well mixed. Cover and chill dough at least one hour.

Preheat oven to 350 degrees.

Shape dough into 1-inch balls. Place 2 inches apart on cookie sheets. With thumb, make indentation in center of each cookie (edges may crack slightly). Fill each indentation with about 1/4 teaspoon jam and top with a pecan.

Bake 12-14 minutes or until edges are lightly browned. Let stand 1 minute; remove from cookie sheet. Cool completely.

Meanwhile, in a small bowl, whisk together all glaze ingredients until smooth. Drizzle over cookies. Place cookies in the refrigerator to firm up the glaze before serving.

Cranberry Vanilla Chip Cookies
Makes 4 dozen

1/2 cup butter, softened
1 1/3 cups sugar
2 eggs
1/2 teaspoon salt
1 3/4 cups flour
1 cup rolled oats
1 1/2 teaspoons baking soda
2/3 cup white chocolate chips
1 cup dried cranberries

In a large bowl, combine butter and sugar beating until light and fluffy. Add eggs. Add flour, oats, baking soda and salt; mix well. Stir in cranberries and chips. Refrigerate dough for at least 1 hour prior to baking.

Preheat oven to 350 degrees. Spray cookie sheets with nonstick cooking spray.

Drop dough by tablespoonfuls 2 inches apart onto cookie sheets. Bake 11-13 minutes or until edges are golden brown. Cool 1 minute before removing from cookie sheets.

Ruby's Favorite Chocochip Cookies
Makes 4 dozen cookies

3 *2 1/4 cups flour*
1 teaspoon baking soda
1 teaspoon salt
1 cup butter, softened
3/4 cup sugar
3/4 cup brown sugar
1 teaspoon vanilla
2 eggs
1 – 1 *1/2 cup chocolate chips*
1 cup nuts (optional)

Preheat oven to 350 degrees.

In a small bowl, combine flour, soda and salt. In a large bowl, cream butter, sugars and vanilla. Add eggs, one at a time, beat well after each addition. Gradually beat in flour mixture. Stir in chocolate chips and nuts.

Drop by rounded tablespoonful onto ungreased cookie sheet. Bake 11-13 minutes until golden brown.

Oatmeal Coconut Fun Chippers

Makes 3 dozen cookies

1 1/2 cups firmly packed brown sugar
1 cup margarine or butter, softened
1 tablespoon milk
1 tablespoon vanilla
2 eggs
2 1/4 cups all-purpose flour
2 teaspoons baking powder
1 teaspoon baking soda
1/2 teaspoon salt
2 cups rolled oats
1 cup coconut
1 (10-ounce) package multicolored candy-coated chocolate chips
Or
1 1/2 cups semisweet chocolate chips

Preheat oven to 350 degrees.

In a large bowl, beat brown sugar and margarine until light and fluffy. Add milk, vanilla and eggs; blend well. Stir in flour, baking powder, baking soda and salt; mix well. Stir in oats, coconut and chocolate chips.

Drop dough by rounded tablespoonfuls 2 inches apart onto ungreased cookie sheets. Bake 9-13 minutes or until light golden brown. Cool 1 minute; remove from cookie sheets. Cool completely.

Note: Cookies made with old-fashioned rolled oats have a moister, coarser texture than those made with quick oats.

Grandma's Kitchen Sink Cookies

Makes 3-4 dozen cookies

1 cup butter, softened
1/2 cup sugar
1/2 cup packed brown sugar
2 eggs
1 teaspoon vanilla
2 cups flour
1 teaspoon baking soda
1/2 teaspoon baking powder
1/2 teaspoon salt
2 cups rolled oats
2 cups chocolate chips
1 cup flaked coconut
1 cup raisins
1 cup chopped walnuts

Preheat oven to 350 degrees. Grease cookies sheet with Pam.

In a large bowl, mix butter and sugars until smooth and creamy. Beat in eggs, one at a time, until well blended. Stir in vanilla.

In a medium bowl, sift together flour, soda, powder, and salt. Stir into butter mixture until well blended. Add oats, chips, coconut, raisins, and walnuts; stir until well blended.

Drop by tablespoonfuls onto greased cookies sheet. Bake 16-18 minutes. Cool on pan for 2 minutes before moving to wire rack to cool completely.

Oatmeal Chocolate Chip Cookies

Makes about 3 dozen cookies

1 3/4 cups all-purpose flour
1 teaspoon baking soda
1/2 teaspoon salt
1 cup butter, softened
1 1/4 cups packed light brown sugar
1/2 cup granulated sugar
2 eggs
2 tablespoons milk
2 teaspoons vanilla extract
2 1/2 cups oats (quick or old-fashioned)
2 cups chocolate chips
1 cup coarsely chopped nuts (optional)

Preheat oven to 350 degrees.

Combine flour, baking soda and salt in a small bowl. Beat butter, brown sugar and granulated sugar in a large bowl. Beat in eggs, milk and vanilla. Gradually beat in flour mixture. Stir in oats, morsels and nuts; mix well.

Drop by rounded tablespoonfuls onto ungreased baking sheets. Bake 12-13 minutes; remove to wire racks to cool completely.

Note: We always place the dough in the refrigerator for at least 2 hours before baking. This helps to keep the cookies compact and chunky.

Snickerdoodles
Makes 4 dozen cookies

1 1/2 cups sugar
1/2 cup margarine or butter, softened
1 teaspoon vanilla
2 eggs
2 3/4 cups all-purpose flour
1/2 teaspoon baking soda
1 teaspoon cream of tartar
1/4 teaspoon salt
2 tablespoons sugar and 2 teaspoons cinnamon, combined

Preheat oven to 350 degrees.

In a large bowl, beat 1 1/2 cups sugar and margarine until light and fluffy. Add vanilla and eggs; blend well. Add flour, cream of tartar, baking soda and salt; mix well.

In a small bowl, combine 2 tablespoons sugar and cinnamon. Shape dough into 1-inch balls; roll in sugar cinnamon mixture. Place 2 inches apart on ungreased cookie sheets.

Bake 8-10 minutes for doughy cookies, 11-13 minutes for firmer cookies. Immediately remove from cookie sheets. Cool completely.

Note: The whimsical name of this cookie originated in New England during the Victorian era. It is a nonsense word for a quickly made confection.

Hors d'oeuvres

Pesto Torta
Serves 16

Pesto:
1/4 cup fresh spinach
1 cup fresh basil
1/2 cup grated Parmesan cheese
1/4 cup walnuts or pine nuts
5 1/2 tablespoons olive oil
Salt and pepper to taste

Filling:
1 pound cream cheese
1 tablespoon lemon juice
2 cloves garlic, minced
Cheesecloth

In a food processor, mix all pesto ingredients to form paste. Using a mixer, beat cream cheese, lemon juice and garlic until smooth.

Cut two 12-inch squares of cheesecloth. Moisten with water; wring dry and lay out flat, one on top of the other. Use cloth to smoothly line a 3-cup mold. With fingers or spatula, spread 1/2 of cheese mixture into mold. Cover with pesto. Top with remaining cheese. Fold ends of cloth over top and press down lightly to compact. Chill 1 1/2 hours or until firm. Invert onto serving tray, remove cheesecloth and garnish with fresh basil leaves. Serve with crackers or vegetables.

Note: Can also be made with Sun Dried Tomato Pesto or purchased pesto to save time.

Hot Shrimp Dip
Makes about 4 cups

16 ounces cream cheese, softened
1 cup mayonnaise
1 pound tiny shrimp
Tabasco sauce, several good shakes, spice to taste
Worcestershire sauce, several good shakes, spice to taste

Preheat oven to 350 degrees. Mix all ingredients together in a baking dish. Bake 30 minutes, until a light brown crust is formed and mixture is hot and bubbly. Serve hot with crusty bread or crackers.

Note: This is so quick and easy and always gets rave reviews!

Low-Cal Dip with a Kick
Makes about 3 cups

2 cups cottage cheese
1 cup grated cheddar cheese
2 tablespoons grated green bell pepper
2 tablespoons grated onion
2 tablespoons prepared horseradish
3 tablespoons mayonnaise
Salt and ground pepper to taste

Combine all ingredients in a medium bowl and mix well. Refrigerate until ready to serve. Serve with crackers, crusty bread or raw vegetables.

Seven-Layer Taco Dip
Serves a crowd

2 avocados, mashed with splash of lemon juice and
   mayonnaise to taste
3 tablespoons sour cream and 3 tablespoons mayonnaise mixed
   with packaged taco seasoning to taste
4 ounces grated Cheddar cheese
4 ounces grated Monterey Jack cheese
3 ounces chopped black olives
2 tomatoes, chopped
4 green onions, chopped

Layer ingredients in a bowl or on a platter in the order given. Serve with tortilla chips.

Note: What would a bed and breakfast in California be, if it didn't serve seafood, artichokes, and Mexican food?

Hearts of Palm Spread
Serves 10

1 (14-ounce) can hearts of palm, drained, finely chopped
3/4 cup Parmesan cheese, grated
3 tablespoons green onion, finely chopped
2/3 cup mayonnaise
1/4 cup sour cream
2 tablespoons pimiento, minced
1/8 teaspoon cayenne

Preheat oven to 350 degrees. Reserve 1 tablespoon each Parmesan cheese and green onion. Mix hearts of palm thoroughly with remaining ingredients. Spread mixture into shallow baking dish. Sprinkle with reserved Parmesan cheese and green onion. Bake 20 minutes or until hot and bubbly. Run quickly under broiler to brown top. Serve with toasted French bread slices or crackers.

Hors d'oeuvres

Baked Brie

Serves 16

Pesto:
Use recipe from Pesto Torta, page 87, or purchased pesto

Puff pastry, (homemade or frozen), 12 x 12-inch sheet
1 pound wheel of brie
1 egg white, beaten

Preheat oven to 350 degrees.

Using the pesto recipe from the Pesto Torta, spread a thick layer of pesto over the top of a one pound wheel of brie. Place pesto-side-down on pastry and fold dough over firmly to secure. Extra pastry can be used to decorate the top.

Brush with egg white and bake about 30 minutes, until golden brown. Cool for a minimum of 30 minutes before serving. Serve with crackers.

Note: For smaller amounts, just cut the brie to the size you want and trim the puff pastry so that there is not an excessive amount on the bottom. Be sure to seal all creases, otherwise the brie will leak out of the pastry.

Hot Artichoke Dip

Yield: 8 cups

3 (10-ounce) cans artichoke hearts, fresh or frozen (not marinated),
drained and coarsely chopped
1 1/2 cups mayonnaise (do not use reduced fat mayonnaise)
1 cup grated Swiss cheese
1/2 cup grated or shredded Parmesan cheese plus some to
top serving dish
1 clove garlic

Preheat oven to 350 degrees.

Combine all ingredients in a 1 quart casserole. Top with shredded Parmesan cheese.

Bake for 30 minutes. Keep warm when serving. Serve with crackers, veggies or crusty bread.

Note: We make this ahead and separate it into smaller serving sizes to freeze. Just take out what you need, thaw and bake.

Ham Spirals
Makes about 40 spirals

1 pound imported boiled ham
8 ounces cream cheese, softened
1 red onion, chopped
Parsley, dried or fresh, chopped

Mix together cream cheese, red onion and enough chopped parsley for color. Spread each slice of boiled ham with cream cheese mixture. Roll each slice starting at short end. Cut each ham roll into 3 or 4 pieces. Secure with a decorative colored toothpick. Arrange on a pretty tray to serve.

Bleu Ribbon Dip
Makes 1 1/2 cups

8 ounces bleu cheese, crumbled
2 cloves garlic, crushed
1/2 cup olive oil
2 tablespoons red wine vinegar
1 tablespoon lemon juice
1/2 cup red onion, chopped
1/2 cup parsley, minced
1/4 teaspoon black pepper

Combine all the ingredients and spread into a shallow dish. Refrigerate for at least one hour or up to 2 days. Serve with baguette slices, crackers or fresh vegetables.

Note: This is a great make-ahead appetizer and is a hit with our guests.

Chunky Seafood Dip
Serves about 30 people

1 pound cooked, peeled, veined shrimp, chopped
16 ounces crab meat (or imitation crab)
16 ounces cooked scallops
6 ounces marinated artichoke hearts, drained and chopped
1 large cucumber, peeled, seeded and chopped
1-2 cups sour cream (add to desired consistency)
1 tablespoon mayonnaise

Combine all ingredients in a large bowl and refrigerate until serving. Serve in mini pastry shells or with bread and crackers.

Note: This is a very versatile dip: it just depends upon the seafood you have and the number of people you want to serve. The dominant flavors should be cucumber and sour cream, so use mayonnaise sparingly.

Hors d'oeuvres

Hot Salmon Dip
Makes 8 cups

1 (14.75-ounce) can salmon
1/4 pound mushrooms, chopped fine
1/2 bunch green onions, chopped
1/2 bunch parsley, chopped
1/2 yellow onion, chopped fine
1 1/2 cups Cheddar cheese, grated
1/2 cup Swiss cheese, grated
1/4 cup water chestnuts, chopped
1 1/2 cups mayonnaise
Pinch of cayenne
Salt and pepper to taste

Preheat oven to 350 degrees.

Sauté onions and mushrooms until soft. Set aside to cool.

In a bowl, mix the rest of the ingredients, except salmon. Add onions and mushrooms and gently stir in salmon. Spoon into an 8-cup soufflé dish.

Bake 35-40 minutes. Serve with crackers or crusty bread.

Note: Bake the amount you would like to serve and freeze the rest. This dip looks very nice served in a hollowed out round of sourdough bread. It tastes great served cold as well.

Mom's Hot Crab Dip
Makes 25 servings

6 tablespoons butter
2 large shallots, finely chopped
2 tablespoons cornstarch dissolved in 2 tablespoons water
1 cup half-and-half
Salt and white pepper to taste
1/8 teaspoon nutmeg
1 pound crab (or imitation crab)
1/4 cup sherry

Melt the butter in a heavy saucepan, add the shallots and sauté over low heat until soft, but not browned, about 3 minutes. Add the cornstarch mixture and blend well. Slowly add the half-and-half; cook, stirring constantly, until the sauce is thick. Season with salt, pepper and nutmeg. Fold in crab, heat through, and remove from heat.

Just before serving, add the sherry. Serve in a chafing dish with crackers or in mini pastry shells.

Dill Dip with a Twist
Makes 1 1/2 cups

1 cup feta cheese (we use Athenos Feta with Basil and Tomato)
1 cup sour cream
2 tablespoons lemon juice
2 tablespoons green onions, chopped
1 tablespoon parsley, chopped
2 cloves garlic, crushed
2 teaspoons fresh dill (or 1/2 teaspoon dried)
1/4 teaspoon salt
1/8 teaspoon cayenne pepper

Combine all the ingredients in a small bowl and chill for 1-24 hours. Serve with crunchy vegetables.

Note: The feta cheese gives this old standby a new twist!

Artichoke-Spinach Dip
Makes 25 servings

28 ounces artichoke hearts, drained
10 ounces frozen chopped spinach, cooked
1 1/2 cups mayonnaise
1 cup grated Parmesan cheese
1/2 teaspoon granulated garlic
1 finely chopped onion
1/2 teaspoon salt
1/8 teaspoon pepper
1 teaspoon lemon juice

Preheat oven to 350 degrees. Butter a 1 1/2-quart casserole.

Place artichoke hearts in food processor and chop.

Cook spinach according to package directions, drain well and squeeze to remove excess moisture.

Combine artichoke, spinach, mayonnaise, Parmesan cheese, garlic, salt, pepper and lemon juice in a large bowl and mix well. Transfer to casserole dish.

Bake about 35 minutes, until bubbly. Serve hot.

Note: This dip freezes well. Thaw completely before baking.

Index

Continued . . .

Index